IN THE FULLNESS OF TIME

Avis D. Carlson

"... true inspiration and entertainment ..."

Publishers Weekly

"Somebody needs to write from the inside about the experience of aging." says Avis Carlson in introducing her book. And she is uniquely qualified to do just that; in her eighties, she is an author and active spokeswoman for the elderly. She is witty, honest and positive as she encourages aging men and women to develop ego strength and self respect.

In The Fullness Of Time

AVIS D. CARLSON

John Curley & Associates, Inc.

South Yarmouth, Ma.

1979

Library of Congress Cataloging in Publication Data

Carlson, Avis D
    In the fullness of time.

    Large print ed.
    1. Old age. 2. Aging. 3. Retirement.
I. Title.
[HQ1061.C347 1979]   301.43'5   78-12306
ISBN 0-89340-172-2

Published in Large Print by arrangement with Contemporary Books, Inc. in the U.S.A. and Porter, Gould & Dierks for the U.K. and Commonwealth.

Distributed in the U.K. and Commonwealth by Magna Print Books.

Printed in Great Britain

Contents

Introduction

From having been an almost totally neglected subject for scientists and writers, we who are old have suddenly become positively fascinating.

Today everybody seems to study us and write about us. Any self-respecting sociology department, for instance, must offer courses in gerontology taught by professors who must publish. All around the country research agencies, ranging from the National Institutes of Health and the Veterans administration down to the local university, are trying to discover the what and the why of the aging process and whether or not it can be slowed or, just possibly, reversed. Every new finding gets immediate wide coverage in the media.

At the same time there has been an

enormous wave of savage accounts of the way our society treats its elderly poor and of passionate calls for reform. These, too, get coverage, partly because most of them are produced by staff writers for magazines or newspapers, and partly because they grate on the collective conscience. Television and radio have also contributed to the horror stories through "specials."

At the same time each news-gathering medium is delighted to run human interest stories about old people judged to be unusual in being alive above the ears. A loquacious, uninhibited nonagenarian may very well wind up on the talk show circuit. And an oldster going quietly about the business of filling a need in some corner of his community is always good for a feature story if he happens to be discovered.

Of writing about the old there is certainly no lack. Why, then, should I, newly become eighty, take it upon myself to spend some of my necessarily limited time writing about the stage of

life in which I find myself? In the face of all the streaming horror stories and books on "successful aging" and feature stories about the lively oldies, how suppose that there is room for yet another discussion of old age?

My reason is this: almost all of the outpouring – whether reports on various phases of the research now being done on the phenomenon of aging or bitter accounts of our society's way with its elderly poor or half-humorous stories of unusual people judged to have aged "successfully" – have been written by people ranging in age from the late twenties to the middle fifties.

Very little has been written about the the experience of aging, for to do that the writer must have become old. Florida Scott-Maxwell in The Measure of My Days, Dr. Paul Tournier in Learn to Grow Old, Carl Jung in a few passages of his Memories, Dreams, Reflections, Pearl Buck in a magazine article in her last year. But not much more. Simone de Beauvoir's The Coming of Age,

appearing when she was sixty, was written in her fifties when she was still outside and dreading. Dr. Olga Knopf was eighty-five when her The Facts and Fallacies of Growing Old appeared, but it is almost wholly made up of her psychiatric observations of her elderly patients.

Yet surely many old people must have had my experience of spending their youth and middle years dreading old age and then discovering that they wasted a sinful amount of emotional energy; that along with the new aches, pains, and numerous frustrations, life is still as interesting and as full of pleasures and small triumphs as it ever was; that though the children and the mate are gone, we are not lonely; that along with the loss of functions we used to have, some new ones are becoming increasingly available if we have the wit to find them and the will to fit ourselves into them.

Somebody needs to write from the inside about the experience of aging.

It is also my conviction that such writing might help to blunt the general stereotyped picture of us, which in the 1970s is less than accurate because so much of it is based upon the real privation and sufferings of about a fourth of us. The writing has been – and still is – needed to shock the general public into doing more to reduce the miseries of the poorest, loneliest, and most neglected portion of us. But the picture that emerges from the impassioned writing amounts to a stereotype portraying us all as not only poor and lonely, but dull and at least partially senile. So the young avoid us – and who can blame them? If they happen upon an interesting oldster, they say, puzzled and thinking to flatter him, "But you don't seem old."

How early the stereotype becomes effective was recently shown in a study conducted among Maryland children aged 3 to 11. When asked what they knew about old people, the children often gave such answers as, "They have heart attacks at 90 and die." "They have to have canes." "They talk funny." Some of the adjectives applied to the old were "sick," "sad," and "ugly." When asked about growing old themselves, they were appalled. One child said he would be sad because he would be dying soon and wouldn't have "the fun and joy I had when I was little." The stereotype takes root very early.

Its power over adults, even elderly adults, was shown in a 1974 study commissioned by the National Council on Aging. In it the Louis Harris organization did in-depth interviews with 4,254 adults, 2,800 of whom were 65 or older. Harris himself summarized the results of the study as showing that society's view of older people is "a flat and unmitigated libel and downright lie." For instance, 61 percent of the 18 to 64 group thought loneliness to be a serious problem among old people, but only 12 percent of the older people agreed. The real shocker, however, was that well over a third of the older people themselves accepted the verdict pronounced by 63 percent of their juniors (which is to say, by society as a whole) that the elderly feel useless and unneeded. Harris interpreted this to mean that the elderly were saying, "Your bad conscience has convinced us that the plight and lot of older people is well nigh hopeless."

Another important comment by Harris was, "The basic libel is that people are declared dead and useless long before their time. In a society which will be aging dramatically in the next decade, this can be a highly dangerous political fact." (Italics mine.)

And so it can. Like the blacks, Chicanos, homosexuals, and feminists, the old of the seventies have had their "consciousness raised" and are fast becoming a vocal and determined minority – a special interest group. Rather suddenly we are becoming politicized, turning ourselves into a pressure group complete with lobbyists and a national headquarters to call for letters and telegrams at auspicious moments. It is not by accident that every layer of government, from Washington right down to City Hall, has been setting up Commissions (or "Offices") on Aging. Politicians have become keenly aware of us.

They'd better! In 1850 only 2.6 percent of the population was 65 years or older. It is now about 10 percent, and our numbers are increasing faster than those of any other segment of the population. As Harris points out, by the year 2000 we are expected to number 33,000,000, which some demographers think may then be about 15 percent of the population. Beyond all that, and for the practicing politician much more important, the percentage of us who actually get out and vote is highest of the age groups. It is no accident that the Commissions and Offices proliferate and politicians of every persuasion extend themselves to publicize the poverty and isolation of the poorest one-fourth of us and to promise improvement. Gray hair may today be far from considered the "crown of glory" it seemed to the writer of Proverbs, but its owners are rapidly learning to use the levers of political power.

It's high time they should, for the last fifty years have been very rough on them. The worship of youth has intensified. Society has gone urban and the family has gone nuclear, living in apartments and small houses and moving from one part of the country to another so that contact between the generations is often slight. Increasingly, there has been no place in the family for the old and, worse, as sixty-five became the cut-off year, the old have had no function in society. At the same time, the rate of social change has become so accelerated that some of us, particularly those living alone in the "downtowns" of America, appear disorganized and unable to cope, already victims of Future Shock.

During the same fifty-year span, anti-biotics and other new medical procedures have lengthened our lives. Because pneumonia no longer carries us off in a few days, the slow killers – kidney and cardiovascular diseases, cancer, arthritis, and senility – have increasingly become our fate. And because of improved surgical techniques, we survive operations that earlier would not even have been attempted. So we live longer, if not always better.

To top off the picture, the last fifty years have seen the arrival of a new institution, the "nursing home," often no more than a container for a large, terribly unhappy, frequently dehumanized population of vegetating old people, sometimes kept oversedated to make their "care" easier. Next came the flood of writing about the "homes" and their occupants. Eventually the writing will result in better conditions. But meantime, we, the elderly, read it and our fear of our future intensifies. If you think, dear Junior, that your present dread of old age is hard, just try thinking ahead to the possibility of a long stretch in a nursing home, particularly if you happen to know the current monthly fees for a "good" home! Apprehensions about having a long final illness are part of the world we live in.   Nor do those of us on the "right" end of the economic scale get off scot-free. For the well-heeled elderly, another institution has arisen. Located usually in a warm climate, the "retirement center" is often luxurious, always comfortable. In it the old with good or reasonably good incomes sit down to nutritious, well-served meals and cram their days with various devices for amusing themselves. But they don't see many children or young people, and whether they know it or not, they live in a state of segregation, functionless and isolated from the main stream of life.

While the old are beginning to have a new group-solidarity and to translate it into lobbying, almost none of us have sat down and tried to analyze the essential qualities of the stage of life into which we have moved. When elderly wits like

Groucho Marx and Goodman Ace get together, they may mourn their decline in bed and at table, but none of them have moved beyond derisive comments about the low estate into which they have fallen.

The statistics and the gerontological information spilling from the laboratories are important, but they make no attempt to convey the experience of old age. Yet if the young and the middle-aged are to understand not only us but their own future prospects, they need to know what it is like to be old in the mid-1970s. Some of us should descibe it, not as scientists do or as journalists and lobbyists and politicians do, but simply as one trying to describe the debits and credits inherent in being old.

My qualifications for the under-taking are, first and most important, the state of being what anybody would call "old." In addition, I must surely have one of the largest and most talkative collections of elderly relatives, in-laws, and friends in existence. I have also barged into a good many Senior Citizen Centers and talked with whomever would suffer me. During the last few years I have done so much reading, clipping, and note-taking that my file cases are crammed. And, for good measure, I am still a modestly functioning part of my neighborhood and city, in constant contact with the young and middle-aged.

But beyond all that, in the course of those activities, I have (or think I have) attained a new composure about my coming death. If the molecular biologists succeed in their hunt for the secrets of aging, they will in the process probably discover how to prolong productive life. It is my belief that if they become able to increase the normal life expectancy by 15 to 20 years, they will have let loose the greatest revolution the human race has ever had to adjust to. Even with a greatly slowed birthrate, the population will expand fantastically and will get radically out of what we now think of as age balance. Just when the planet's resources are dwindling, new opportunities for productive lives will have to be multiplied in order to provide scope for all the new energy unloosed upon the world. The whole system of education will have to be overhauled. The economic and environmental problems will be staggering. And all the while, simply because of our growing numbers, the elderly will be growing more politically powerful than we are now.

Maybe this new body of energetic seniors would cope imaginatively and wisely with all the new governmental, economic, international, and social problems. Maybe. But, historically, the elderly have no reputation for innovations. Historically, the young have forced change while the old stood by and urged caution.

In my lifetime I have seen so much change that I tend to be gun-shy, for it always seems to bring evil as well as good. From having lived under the blue skies and simple technologies of the Kansas Flint Hills, I have seen the pollution and social dislocations and reckless consumption of the earth's supply of fossil fuel. I have had to learn (sort of) to live with the nuclear bomb. I know all too well that medical advances may doom me to years of vegetation. I'm not sure how much more change I wish to adapt myself to. Therefore I am willing to forego the extra years the scientists are working toward. But not just out of chicken-heartedness. I believe that enough is already known, or is presently being hammered out to allow us to have lives as full of love and interest as they ever were. What I am not willing to accept is the way so many of my contemporaries either take themselves out or are pitched out of social function, and indeed out of their humanity, simply because they have grown old.

Somebody should be pointing out how hard it is to maintain a feeling of self-worth in a society that worships youth and considers the old not only useless and burdensome, but boring. And still worse, in a society in which almost everybody over forty lives in profound dread of his own approaching old age. Such a society may have some guilt feelings about shoving old people into any convenient corner and forgetting them, except for handing out Social Security and Medicare payments. But it continues with the shoving, partly because we remind younger people of their own future fate. How can such a society believe that old age is simply a phase of life, like infancy, like adolescence, like maturity? That it, like all the others, has its own special brood of struggles, pains, fears, and frustrations – but also its own set of pleasures and joys, some of which attended all the preceding stages, but some belonging only to the last?

At this point my thinking becomes very personal. Do I myself honestly believe that this last stage of life can be a good experience?

At the moment it is, for I am still

mobile and, like many people my age nowadays, still fully engaged with life. But if I live five, or even ten more years, my body, and perhaps my mind, will inevitably have deteriorated. Will I then be able to accept that condition of life?

Who knows? Certainly not I. But then I never did know what the next five years would do to me or what I would do with them.

In The Fullness Of Time

Part I

1

The Minuses of Old Age

Although I completely believe that old age can be a time of learning and growing, no one with two grains of sense would try to deny that this final stage of life has some very bad minuses. For none of us is it a rose garden. For many of us it is a time of real torment.

So, before we go on to the pluses, let's lay out the debits honestly instead of trying to slip over them as many sentimentalists have done throughout history.

As the study with Maryland children showed, dread of old age runs deep – and begins early. Sometimes quite small children come to a sudden, devastating realization that they will some day look like the grandparents who seem to them

3

unspeakably ancient. I myself was one of those children and the experience was sufficiently traumatic to stay with me during all the ups and downs of life.

My mother's mother was a delicately boned little Kentuckian who was never made for the Kansas frontier on which she spent her adult life. She had been asthmatic from childhood, in a time when even the word "allergic" was unknown, much less all the drugs and immunologic therapies available to today's sufferers. Consequently, because she was so often sick, she was very thin, and because her asthma seemed to be worse outdoors, her skin almost transparently blue-white.

One day, when I was perhaps six or seven years old, I happened to notice her hands. They were, I know now, the hands of a sick, prematurely aged woman. The outline of every bone was plainly visible; some of the finger joints had begun to gnarl; the blue veins stood out and crawled just under the paper-thin skin like worms, I thought with a

4

childish shudder.

On an impulse I put my plump, brown, and probably dirty hand up beside hers. The contrast has stayed with me.

"Grandma," I asked in what was no doubt a very small voice, "Will my hands ever look like yours?"

"That will depend partly on how well you are," she answered. "But yes, I think in time they will probably look something like mine."

The shock was overwhelming. I looked at her two hands and tried to imagine what it would be like to carry around such repulsive looking objects. Then I looked at her familiar face and noticed for the first time that her gray hair was very thin, that her forehead had deep horizontal lines, that her cheeks were sunken, that, because she had neglected to put in her "false teeth," her mouth was a small depression in her face.

"You mean I'm going to get old some day?" I asked in the carefully casual way of a child who has something important on his mind.

"Yes, Avis, if you live long enough, you will some day be old."

It happened that the rather recent death of my grandfather, her husband, had given me my first introduction to death for human beings. As a farm child I had known, of course, that pets and animals die, but that people also died had somehow failed to soak in on me. So my next question was really important.

"You mean I have to die someday?"

By this time she undoubtedly wished me home with my mother, but she did not flinch. "Yes, Honey, you will someday die and go to live with God. Like your grandfather."

That was really too much. I got out of there in a hurry and, so far as I can remember, never again engaged an adult in that sort of conversation. In fact, I locked the question of impending old age and death so tightly within myself that I forgot the whole episode until recently when I began to write about growing old. But it no doubt expressed itself every time my forty- or fifty- or sixty-year-old self quailed on observing a new sign of oncoming old age. (As still happens!)

I might think the incident was unique, the result of a particular set of circumstances happening to a particular child, except for something that happened years later, when I was teaching a course in magazine journalism. One day I was in need of a springboard for discussing the importance of cultivating the habit of observation. On an impulse that may have gone back to the childhood experience and its repression, I asked my students to write a paragraph or two describing the hands of old people.

To my utter amazement nearly all of those young people, aged eighteen to twenty-one, sat there and from memory turned in very creditable descriptions of aged hands. This could only mean that they had thought about the physical evidences of old age – may even have had something like my experience. So perhaps it was not so unique after all. In our culture a distaste for the prospect of becoming old is part of the very air we breathe.

Nor is this distaste for the final stage of life peculiar to the twentieth century. The several columns of fine print in the Bartlett index devoted to quotations about old age show that hardly any writers from Homer to W. H. Auden have found anything desirable about it. Cicero and Marcus Aurelius and the Chinese sages did, of course. But after them, who? Victor Hugo could remark with Gallic chivalry, "When grace is joined with wrinkles, it is adorable." But Homer's famous tribute, "a green old age, unconscious of decay," applied only to a supermortal, Odysseus. When Lowell conceded that old age may have some "reverend graces of its own as good in their way as the noisy impertinence of childhood, the elbowing self-conceit of youth, or the pompous mediocrity of middle life,"[1] one notes that he could

1. From A Good Word for Winter

only praise old age by listing the very worst qualities of the earlier stages of life.

The ancient writer of Proverbs could proclaim confidently that "a hoary head is a crown of glory if it is gained in righteousness," but one of his countrymen said sadly of the hero, Joshua, "he was stricken in years" – "stricken" being, of course, synonymous with "afflicted."

In general and throughout most of history, the popular picture of an aged person has been of a doddering, dim-witted, absurdly opinionated creature beset with aches and pains. Who wouldn't be badly put off by the idea that he is inevitably coming to that? Especially when he knows (or thinks he does) that even this gloomy picture of his coming state does not tell the whole story, which is that with every passing week he will be "more so," until finally, in the famous words of Shakespeare, he enters the Seventh Age:

Second childishness, and mere
  oblivion,
Sans teeth, sans eyes, sans taste,
  sans everything.

For three and a half centuries these words have haunted humanity. Unfortunately they are not, even today, just a grisly Shakespearean fantasy. One can see their embodiment while walking the corridors of almost any nursing home and glancing through open doors. The pathetic, shrunken figures huddled in chairs or stretched out on beds are of those who are "sans everything" but breath. All that is left for them is the final drop into the Unknown. They have become an important part of our stereotypical picture of old age.

No wonder, then, that distaste for the very idea of becoming old is bone-deep among us and well nigh universal. Beginning in childhood, it probably intensifies with each decade after the third.

Children have so much bounce and so

much openness to all the stimuli crowding in upon them that they rarely give more than fleeting attention to what is happening to their grandparents – in fact, they may not even notice it unless they happen to have an experience like mine.

Adolescents have too many personal problems, too many ravening anxieties, to think much about what lies at the far end of what to them seems like limitless time. In a period of life when every disappointment is crushing and every defeat seems final, they simply lack the emotional energy to imagine themselves ever becoming old. Most of them have difficulty imagining themselves as an elderly thirty, let alone seventy-five. If noticed at all, the behavior of grandparents seems merely the personal perculiarities, either quaint or outrageous, of Gramp or Gram.

But by thirty most people have begun to have at least occasional intimations, not of immortality, but of most earthy mortality. By this time, if grandparents and great-grandaunts or uncles are still around, they are old, and the thirty-year-old cannot avoid knowing that it will eventually happen to him. The state of old age is waiting out there somewhere, frightening and repulsive.

But aging, like dying, is something a person can get good at not thinking about. Throughout all the busy, harried middle years, when people are holding jobs, bringing up families, shouldering community responsibilities and otherwise doing the world's work, the dread of what lies ahead becomes keener – if and when they allow themselves to think about it. But accepted or unaccepted, by age forty-five the intimations are usually a fact of life. The first gray hairs have appeared, and children have begun to leave home. Bifocals have probably had to be accepted or at least are on the horizon. Women find themselves beleaguered by hot flashes and kindred hormonal discomforts. Most men find their hairline slipping badly. Waistlines have begun to be a problem for both sexes, and doctors have taken to dreary discussions of diet and exercise.

Although I myself had all the intimations that usually come to women, the first really sharp stab came one evening in my late forties at a symphony concert. Suddenly in a very high, soft passage, the hands of the violinists began to float up and down – up and down. Like butterflies – and as silently. I had had my first warning that the family trait of nerve deafness was in my genes and had begun to manifest itself by washing out high frequency tones.

Later that distressing night I remembered a little poem written years earlier by an acquaintance when she was in her late forties. The poem described her emotion on observing how much she was getting to look like her mother during the latter's last years. I cannot remember the whole poem, but the final lines were:

I could not tell
Whether I wept for the woman who was dead

Or the woman from whom youth
had fled.

I did not weep, but I certainly felt like
it. (And now, as every year intensifies
this deafness, which hearing aids do not
much help, I find it increasingly hard to
function in groups.)

By fifty it has become more difficult
for us to ignore what is relentlessly going
on, however slowly. A practiced person
can do pretty well at ignoring it, but even
he has moments of seeing. What he does
to counter the process depends somewhat on his temperament, but mostly on
his income. He may take the common-
sense tack that aging is a natural process
and who is he to try to beat the game. But
if he has the income (and perhaps if he
doesn't), he will probably elect to fight
the process. Because, if he is ever going
to be affluent, he has reached that glad-
some stage by his fifties, the decade when
he is most likely to adopt some of the
rejuvenating procedures long practiced
by actors.

Consequently, so the feature writers tell us, face-lifts have become commonplace. Once almost exclusively limited to women and actors, plastic surgery is on the increase among men. A recent Associated Press story from Rio de Janeiro says that twenty percent of the face-lifts now being done in that city are performed on men. This, of course, is in addition to all the surgery that has resulted from the discovery that hair can be transplanted as successfully as young cabbages!

All across the country classes in yoga are attracting both men and women who hope to keep their joints usable or to limber up those that have already stiffened. Diet books in never-ending procession become best sellers – and cholesterol has become a dirty word.

People under none of the pressures that affect the world of show business are having their front teeth capped to the tune of several hundred dollars a tooth. Every city has its expensive health and beauty salons with their impressive array of program directors, exercise machines, special baths, and "facial specialists." Although the clientele is still mostly female, it is becoming increasingly male. In fact, the whole youth and beauty industry has more and more male patrons. It is still women who have silicone implants and stand in pathetic hopefulness at cosmetic counters watching demonstrations of moisturizers, hormone creams, and eye creams. But, no doubt about it, men are gingerly joining the ranks of old age warriors.

Far be it from me to downgrade the war. Though I was never much involved in it, my reasons were not of the purest. First, I begrudged laying out for cosmetics what might have gone into books. Second, since the ripe age of thirteen I have known that whatever I was to get out of life would not be had because of my looks. Further, from infancy forward I was blessed with a lack of passion for fattening food. Hence, I'm fairly sure that I've faced the bogey with

16

no more than average suffering. But even so, I am saddened when I observe the deteriorations taking place in my body and mind. I sometimes tell saleswomen who are bringing on sleeveless dresses that I've reached a stage in life where the more of me that is covered up the better I look. They laugh and I laugh, but the shriveled arms and legs are not funnier than the sagging face, even to those of us who try to be philosophic about them. (Nor is the fact that the most delicious moment of the whole day is the one when the hot shower first strikes the night-stiffened arthritic neck and shoulders.)

For me, however, the physical manifestations of age are the least of its distresses, much easier borne than the lapses of memory that plague me oftener as the years pile up. Sir Walter Scott is said to have confessed that he received a letter, carefully wrote out an answer, then began to search for the bit of paper containing his correspondent's address but by that time had mislaid the letter! I can thoroughly sympathize, because it often seems to me that I spend half my time looking for something I "just laid down."

I am made ashamed by this tendency and frequently admonish myself; "Remember this, will you!" But the beratings and admonitions seem to avail me little. When occasionally I stand before an open refrigerator door trying to remember what I came for, I am embarrassed – and if anybody happens to be looking at me, I am humiliated. Even though I try to pass off the situation as a joke, some part of my psyche bleeds a little. Younger people try to console me by saying they do the same thing, but I remember that I used to swing open a refrigerator door and confidently snatch out what I wanted, just as I once skipped through a book and remembered practically every detail of its contents. No matter how we joke about it, it is humiliating to start a sentence and then find that a commonly used word has absolutely disappeared for the moment.

Old age actually is a hard thing to face and as such needs to be treated like any fearsome thing that haunts and frightens: brought out into the open, looked in the face, talked about freely, laughed at if possible.

For such therapy all the horror stories now being written about the inhuman life and routines in some nursing homes are no help what ever. In fact, the dread feeds upon such stories and becomes harder to cope with as they multiply. The possibility of having to wear out a lengthy stay in a "home" is, I am convinced, now an element in the general fear of old age. Among the elderly even the "good" homes are feared because they are so expensive that "my money will run out if I linger a long time." Many of today's old deny themselves experiences they would enjoy and benefit from, such as travel or enter-tainment, because they feel they must hoard their resources against the contingency of a long terminal illness.

The 1974 Report of the Senate Subcommittee on Long Term Care could only increase their fears. Some of the Committee's findings were: that a million old people were then being cared for in nursing homes; that the average monthly charge was $600 (inflation has now greatly increased that figure); that there were three times as many homes as hospitals, but only about 15 percent as many registered nurses working in the homes; that between 50 percent and 80 percent of all nursing home patients die there; that most nursing home patients were mentally impaired and unable to walk; that inspections by state enforcement agencies were "generally a fraud."

This report simply cannot avoid intensifying the common dread of aging. Of course, that is not to say that such stories shouldn't be printed. Reforms never come without emotion-rousing publicity.

What this means to me is that even while the reforms are being passionately sought, the specter must be perceived and dealt with, because sooner or later every human being is going to be affected by it, either personally or through someone he loves. We need not be ashamed of our dread, for it is realistic: more than half of us will probably spend our last days in a nursing home.

Old age is followed by death, and even if he has turned one hundred, no healthy person really wants to die. We have a right to feel somewhat apprehensive about aging. But it is simply absurd to spend thirty years either denying it will come or quaking at the thought of it.

2

Some Common Strategies for Dealing with the Specter

The outer marks of our elderly condition are, after all, not so very numerous. Any oldster or his middle-aged children can tick them off readily: thinning gray hair, deepening facial lines, impaired digestion, painful or at least stiffening joints, failing sense organs, increasing aches and pains, decreasing muscular strength – and so on down the line of physical symptoms. The list is not the same for all of us, but we nearly all have some chronic disease and we collect more as we go along. Luckily, the deteriorations usually come on so gradually that we are not as much upset by them as we might be if they came on suddenly and all together, as in the case of a stroke.

We may not be as aware of our mental and emotional symptoms of aging as we are of the physical, but our children would have no difficulty in tallying them: failing memory, rigidity, a growing tendency to "repeat" or to withdraw, perhaps a new drift toward petulance and self-pity that may verge on downright "orneriness" – or in some individuals of advanced age, a beautiful new tranquility. (And how these last cases are treasured by younger people and lauded by the world's writers!)

The symptoms may be pretty much the same, but the way we deal with our old age, how we experience it, is a very personal matter, depending partly on our temperament, education, income, religious beliefs, and the circumstances we have encountered during our long voyage. To illustrate the differences, let me quote from nine elderly people, all relatives or close friends of mine, none of them either rich or pinched by poverty. In formal education they range from almost none through college degrees to on Ed.D.

1. The first was an aunt in her early seventies. "The trouble with old age," she wrote in the thin, wavering script of one in the early stages of Parkinson's disease, "is that you can only fight a delaying action. You can't hope to win."
In her prime she had been a powerful woman who could do housework all day and then talk all night if she found someone interesting and willing to stay up with her in a conversational binge. What she was saying was, "Fight it with all you have, even though you know you can't win." If she had lived to read them, she would have gloried in Dylan Thomas's lines:

Do not go gentle into that good night,
Old age should burn and rave at close
    of day;
Rage, rage against the dying of the
    light.

She was not one of those who fight the

24

look of old age. Nobody cared less about that than she, though she did occasionally go on a three-day fast in order to lose some weight. No moisturizers or even rouge ever sat on her dresser. What she fought were old age itself and the encroachments it brought through her disease.

Millions of elderly Americans take her way. They are the Old Age Warriors, stuffing themselves with vitamins, joining Weight-Watcher groups, experimenting with exercise programs and hormone cosmetics, going faithfully for the annual rite of checkup, having their hair tinted or buying wigs. If they are sufficiently affluent, they may try a hair transplant, a facelift, or a sojourn at a health and beauty spa.

They get results, too. The middle class and affluent elderly of today are a much better looking and acting set of people than the old people I knew in my parents' generation. They really are "younger" than their parents were at the same age. But they can only partly and temporarily win. They can fight and postpone old age, but as my aunt said, they "can't hope to win." Unless and until the molecular biologists succeed in ferreting out the secrets of aging itself and thereby become able to "set back the biological time-clock," we are only going to be able to battle and postpone.

2. "The trouble with old age," commented an ironic friend in his mid-seventies who was plagued with glaucoma and a capricious heart, "is that the prospects are so poor." He was saying, "Old age is a bad business with a worse future, but joking about it helps me put up with it." (On another occasion he said it was "hell" with plenty of emphasis and an oral exclamation point.)

Most oldsters take this tack at least occasionally. Some settle into it like a protective coat. My husband, for one, became quite proficient with it. "There are four stages in life," he used to wisecrack, "childhood, youth, middle age, and the 'you're looking good' stage." In this little joke he was protesting the smugness with which younger men tell their elders, "You're looking good." On other occasions he would quip, "There are four stages in life – infancy, youth, middle age, and – let's see now – I forget what the other one is." Or he would ask with mock seriousness, "Why is it that just when you've learned the answers, nobody asks you any questions?"

One has only to walk into the nearest senior citizen center to hear the tired "old-timer" or "grandma" jokes. If these wheezes didn't seem to help armor us, they would not be in such common use. Whatever one can laugh at can be more easily tolerated. When asked how he liked being old, Maurice Chevalier is credited with one of his best sallies, "Considering the alternative, I like it fine, thank you."

By our sixties most of us have begun to laugh at any untoward incident and proclaim that we are "slipping." Actually, at least in the early stages of the game, we don't really believe it and expect our listeners to reply politely that they don't see any signs of dotage. If they don't so reply, we are apt to feel let down and wonder if they didn't say it because they couldn't.

3. "Everything's wrong with old age." grumbled an uncle bitterly. "Mother and I took care of our old people, and we didn't bellyache about it either." He was ninety, very deaf, and badly crippled. He was also one of a multitude of bewildered, resentful old people in nursing homes. His infirmities were serious and his disposition not the world's easiest. His daughter and daughters-in-law were modern women with lives and paychecks of their own. His way is, unfortunately, the one taken by an army of oldsters who believe, often with complete justice, that life and off-spring have dealt unfairly with them. So they make no effort to find friends

among the other residents, whom they regard as "loony" or at best totally uninteresting. Instead, they nurse a load of resentment, which makes things more difficult for themselves, their families, and those hired to care for them. A vicious circle thus builds up. The louder the complaints, the less affection and emotional support come to the old person at a time of life when he needs both more desperately than at any time since infancy. The sons and daughters may write or visit faithfully, but the parent is not fooled – he knows very well that only a sense of duty pushes them. So neither he nor they get any real pleasure from the letters or the visits. In nursing homes one can watch the attendants brace themselves when they enter his room – and one can suspect that at least part of the oversedation often resorted to in the poorer "homes" is a defense against irascible complaining.

4. "I'm no use to anyone, sitting here in a wheelchair," mourned my mother-

in-law times innumerable. "I'm a burden on the family and I don't see why God leaves me here." Her plan is often used, and it yields some real rewards for all the old people who take it. When she bewailed being "useless and a burden," her listener always answered by pointing out the important ways in which she still served us – which, of course, she loved to hear. But the manner of her death told us that she hadn't really wanted to die. At well past ninety-six she had such a severe stroke that her doctor said she could not live through the weekend. But she lingered for six weeks – and on her own strength, without any of the hospital life-prolonging machines. She may have consciously thought she wanted to die, but her unconscious and her body thought otherwise. Her wheelchair had become a protection against the demands life is always making on us to change, to adapt ourselves to altered circumstances. Even the final change was resisted to the bitter end.

While judging that her strategy was a

mistake, one must grieve that the hardships of repeated childbearing amid the brutal deprivations of the Western Kansas frontier were so grinding that the wheelchair came to be a refuge. She was a sensitive, natively gifted person whom life used very badly. And she lived in a time and place where there were no good doctors and before there were any psychotherapists, or even any clergymen trained in counseling.

Many old people use her plan with less excuse. They earnestly proclaim that they want to die, that they are useless and a burden and they wish they were out of it all, enjoying the future existence their religion promises them after death. A few of them may actually be so deeply depressed that they really do long for exit. But for most of them, most of the time, it is not much more than a way of expressing their dissatisfaction with the way things have shaped up for them. From having been so useful as to feel indispensable, they have come to feel useless – about as severe a comedown as a human being could have. Indeed, some scientists now feel that undiagnosed chronic depression may be a larger factor than organic brain disease in personality deterioration of the old.

5. My mother was a completely different type. When she was sixty-three and fighting an illness that had seemed to be minor, she said, "If it's going to be like this the rest of the way out, so that I can't do any of the things I want to do, I don't care how soon it's over." Three weeks later she was gone.

This kind of person simply refuses the limitations of old age. They do not "commit suicide" – would never do that. They merely refuse to be "cabined, cribbed, and confined." One often sees this sort of reaction in the old who have become newly widowed. What is left of life does not seem to them worth the hard struggle to build a new pattern of living – which is probably why so many die within a few weeks or months of the partner's death. Especially if the relationship has been very close or if the bereaved is in poor health, he (or more likely, she) just may not be able to summon up the strength required to create a new life.

Some elderly people who see themselves condemned to a life of invalidism also do not make the effort required to absorb the cruel limitations. And so they more or less consciously relinquish life, perhaps by refusing food, perhaps by not seeking medical help when they should, perhaps in one of the mysterious ways in which spirit rules body. Some of these people, like my mother, have been among the most ardent lovers of life, and they cannot submit to its dwindling down to a miserly trickle.

6. Another kind of old person entirely is a brother-in-law who is – I choose the word carefully – addicted to travel. At eighty-seven his plan for dealing with old age is to ignore it. All his life he has been restless and ready to move on from

wherever he happened to be. Since his retirement he has been almost constantly off either to visit one of his children or grandchildren scattered across the nation or just to see a part of the country he has not seen before. If not on a trip he is planning where to go next. Perhaps this restlessness is part of his Viking inheritance – as my husband's brother, his name is Carlson!

"As long as I can climb into a bus or onto a plane," he could well announce, "I'm going to go. I can't drive anymore, but the buses and planes go and my children take me with them sometimes. If my unreliable ticker stops someday when I'm away from home, so be it. Meantime, I'm going to go just as long as there are people and places I want to see and money to take me." I never heard him use those exact words, but he lives them. I have heard him say, "I'm never going to be old. I don't feel old and I'm not going to act old."

He is one of the elders who believe that we get old by "thinking old," which he is determined not to do. Like a host of others, he believes that people "hypnotize themselves right into old age." If he ever chanced to read one of Beauvoir's quotes from Gide's Journal, I know what he would say, The quotation is:

I scarcely feel my age, and although every hour of the day I tell myself, "My poor old fellow, you are seventy-three and more," I cannot really persuade myself of it.

"That's exactly what I'm talking about," he would snort. "Telling himself every hour that he is old. Nuts! Of course he will get old if he takes that road." (At this point I cannot resist remarking that Gide's way is taken by many of us. We don't feel old, but we keep reminding ourselves and commiserating with ourselves on the passage of the years.)

Not my brother-in-law. When it came time to surrender his driver's license, he took to the buses and planes. He has no part in any community organization except for an occasional chore for the American Association of Retired Persons. He sincerely feels that all his long working years entitle him to freedom from community responsibilities. And, anyway, he doesn't enjoy organizations and he means to "enjoy these last years" by doing what he likes to do best.

7. Another brother-in-law takes a different tack. "I refuse to be categorized as old. I don't enjoy most of the old people I meet and so I associate with them as little as I can. I'll never go near a senior citizen center." As he spoke he was a well-preserved seventy-three sending his Chrysler down an interstate highway at a good clip. When his wife was alive she organized and managed their social life. Now that she is gone, he keeps his house, has dinner one night a week at the Country Club, attends his church, escorts a widow friend considerably younger than he, goes to

the Colorado mountains for a month's fishing each summer as he has done for the last forty years – and in general lives a comfortable, independent life, enjoying the respect his smallish town gives him as a solid citizen who pays his bills and keeps out of trouble.

All of this is fine for seventy-three, but if he lives to be eighty-three or even ninety-three, his situation will be quite different. Thus far he has been able to avoid the society of the old and to associate with the middle-aged through their common interest in sports and the news of the day. But in ten years everything may well have changed drastically. By then he may have become one of the country's lonely old people. But for the present he sees no reason to identify in any way with the old. He seems to feel that if he keeps his distance from people his own age or older, no one will notice the signs of his own aging.

He is not alone in feeling so. Many seventy and eighty-year-olds choose his way of dealing with the oncoming of old age. In commenting on the death of the octogenarian Missouri painter, Thomas Hart Benton, the NBC evening news quoted him as saying he "wouldn't have anybody over fifty in the house." One wonders how many old people heard and were hurt by the remark. Millions, undoubtedly.

In this connection I recall a conversation of forty years ago. A friend of mine was sputtering because her parents, having moved to her small city in order to be near her during their retirement years, now wanted to incorporate their new social life into hers and her husband's. "They say they enjoy us and our friends more, enjoy our talk and the things we do more than the talk and activities of people their own age. Of course they do. We don't talk about aches and pains because we don't have them yet. And if we want to do gourmet cooking, we still have the stomachs to digest it," she fumed.

It cannot be said too emphatically: Most people just entering old age avoid the company of the old because they don't enjoy it. (To be truthful, almost no one does!) So most oldsters completely understand a friend of mine who, on moving into a retirement apartment, asked herself in stricken amazement, "What am I doing here with all these old people?" Bernard Baruch is supposed to have once said that for him old age was always about fifteen years from where he was at the moment.

The bare fact of having become old is almost unrealizable. We oldsters ought to make the transition easier by assuming responsibility for making a pleasant and rewarding social life for ourselves, one that will be more attractive to the newly or not-quite old. We would also have more fun ourselves.

8. Still another strategy is that followed by my husband and one of my brothers-in-law: "Learn to do something new that other people will admire." (As we shall see, this business of other people's admiration is vastly important

for the old.) For women this "something new" may be exceptional needlecraft or rug-making or weaving or painting or any of a dozen other crafts. But it needs to be good, so as to receive merited attention.

For my husband and brother-in-law the "something new" opened a door to a whole new world. My husband had been developing a city garden for a long time. When he began to see interesting shapes in discarded roots and prunings, he found he could amuse himself and others by exaggerating the shapes with a pocket knife. From there it was natural to study under a wood sculptor, purchase proper tools, and launch out into work that brought him much happiness and some local attention. Soon after retirement the brother-in-law took to going to estate sales and buying up old silver flatware, which he then taught himself to make into interesting jewelry and even silver sculpture. Says he: "I must be the only secondhand silversmith in existence." But people praise his work and buy it.

Both men were following a natural bent that their work lives had not allowed them to develop. At the same time they were opening themselves up to some inherent assets: "good hands" and a puckish sense of humor. But the fact that other people enjoyed their work added greatly to the satisfaction they took in it. They had unearthed for themselves some enormous assets in the "battle for respect" that today's old people must wage.

9. "The way to deal with old age," says a friend who has been a professor of Community Organization at Penn State College, "is to give oneself in volunteer service to those less fortunate. Retirement was no big deal for me. I'm as busy and as happy now as I ever was."

When she retired, she plunged into volunteer work in her community, and among many other activities became the prime mover in the local organization of Meals-on-Wheels and Legal Services for the Poor programs. When she dies, it will probably be in the middle of some committee meeting called to consider ways and means of meeting some community problem that has been in existence from time immemorial but nobody ever bothered with before. She is lucky, of course, in that her professional life fitted her for retirement as a glove fits the hand for which it was sized. She is expert in group dynamics – knowing why a group is succeeding in its undertakings or why it is floundering. She can be patient with a group while it gathers facts. then musters strength to move toward its goals. Long ago she learned how to become a member of an organization while still exerting pressure on it.

With this technical skill Dr. Rose Cologne combines a deep concern over the flaws in American society. She knows and deplores its shortcomings and inequities and, as a practicing Quaker, she is constantly ready to battle suffering or injustice. As a fervent democrat (small d) she passionately believes that ordinary citizens can have an impact on their society and enrich their own lives.

The days and weeks are not long enough for her. Her appointment calendar is crowded. She probably has not had a bored moment since her retirement party. I suspect that she is pioneering in an area that may come to be well peopled by the old of the future. Now that young women are entering the labor market the minute their youngest child enters school (or before!) more and more of the voluntary organizations on which our society has heavily depended are having to rely on newly retired men and women for the necessary leadership posts. For the old, who have all suffered one or more "role losses," the new "volunteerism," which Dr. Cologne has spent her life fostering, offers a prime way to build up our sense of self-worth.

There are probably other ways of dealing with the oncoming of age, but these nine are in general use. Most old people, of course, do not confine themselves to a single plan, but dip now and then into another strategy that accords with their life-styles.

What seven of the nine game plans have in common is their rejection of old age, seeing it as something that happens to other people but must not be permitted to happen to oneself. At least in its early stages it is something to be denied, evaded, ignored, wryly joked about. But when it can no longer be denied, evaded, ignored, or laughed about, too many old people swing to the other extreme and give up, without ever really trying to make anything of their new life situation. Particularly if the old person happens to be basically timid and pessimistic, he may simply tell himself that for him everything is now over, and then settle down to the television and whatever minor distraction happens to come into his day.

It seems that in old age we mostly are what we have been earlier, only more so. The fun-lovers will usually manage to have themselves some fun in spite of the arthritis. Unless transformed by a stroke or arterio-sclerosis, good people will remain kind and generous. The timid and the pessimistic, particularly if they have had both traits, will find all sorts of good reasons for denying themselves pleasant or stimulating experiences. If, for instance, someone proposes a trip they will find excellent reasons for its absolute impossibility; "I don't have the right clothes." "I might get sick while I was away." "I'm afraid to spend the money – I may have a long terminal illness and run out." "My diet is such a nuisance when I'm away from home."

Or, on being offered an opportunity for a volunteer job: "I don't know that I would be able to get there every day." "It's not safe to be out on the streets nowadays." Or any of a hundred other excuses that can be latched onto as a protection against trying something new and unfamiliar.

Particularly if the old person has no younger family members to prod and urge, he may just give up in the name of accepting old age and settle down to drag out his days without ever really trying to make anything of his new situation. This is the old person who tells the same stories time after time and complains drearily about his pains and worries. This of course is also the old person most likely to be lonely. If we vegetate in our houses or before our TVs, we are going to be bored and, consequently, boring. And lonely, because boring people attract few companions. Those who feel some responsibilities for the timid or pessimistic old person should be firm about pushing him out from the walls behind which he has retreated. His game plan is easy, but lethal.

3

We Too Have an Identity Problem

Every literate person is familiar with and probably somewhat bored by Erik Erikson's phrase, "Identity crisis." In the past decade it has been tossed about ad nauseam – with about as many connotations as users. Thus a mother may apologize for a troublesome teenager, "He's having a hard time finding himself." Or if she is especially hip, she may attribute his hard time to "his identity crisis." The teenager himself, if sufficiently verbal, may ask the world to understand how painful it is not to know "who I am." On the other hand, one of my contemporaries has a wicked stock phrase when she sees some young person whose sex is not readily determinable, "That one really has an identity problem."

As commonly used, the phrase applies to youngsters on the threshold of adulthood, or, if there has been some unfortunate blockage in personal development, to young adults. In either case, it applies to the young, who are held to be engaged in a "search for identity."

What has not been so clearly recognized is that entrance into old age, like entrance into adulthood, also sets up an identity criisis, in which the individual becomes uncertain in his image of himself and of the role or roles expected of him. Because so little understood, this uncertainty is one of the hardest features of growing old.

But before we begin to talk about it, let's get a good solid definition of "identity" under our feet. One of the best is, of course, the one formulated by Erikson himself.

In psychological terms, identity formation employs a process of simultaneous reflection and observation, a process taking place on all levels of mental functioning, by which the individual judges himself in the light of what he perceives to be the way in which others judge him in comparison to themselves and to a typology significant to them; while he judges their way of judging him in the light of how he perceives himself in comparison to them **and to types that have become relevant to him. This process is, luckily, and necessarily, for the most part unconscious except where inner conditions and outer circumstances combine to aggravate a painful, or elated, "identity-consciousness."[1] (Italics mine.)**

In short, says Erikson, identity is the result of a constant interplay between ourselves and (a) our thinking about ourselves and (b) what we feel others feel we are or (c) should be. As he also says, this three-fold process mostly takes

1. Erik Erikson, Identity, Youth and Crisis (**New York: W. W. Norton & Co., 1968), pp. 22-23.**

place unconsciously and without too much stress.

It is my observation and, more importantly, my experience that there is an identity crisis attending entrance into old age and that it is every bit as full of uncertainty and emotional distress as the one we went through a half century earlier.

As I watch my adolescent grandchildren it sometimes seems to me that they and I have a great deal in common. (Naturally, they don't think so!) Both they and I are emerging from a familiar stage of life into an unknown one where we must be constantly feeling for a new footing. Both of us belong to an agegroup commonly regarded as a social problem, if not a downright nuisance. Growing up is scary business, but so is growing old. At times childhood seems a poor preparation for the stresses imposed by changes in the bodies and emotions of the adolescent. But believe me, the elder often feels that his past was not a very good preparation for the stresses imposed by his changing body and emotions – not to mention the furiously changing world around him.

But, of course, the analogy can't be pushed very far. There are great differences. The adolescent is changing at a great pace, usually much faster than the one laid out for his grandparents. Within a few years he must have acquired enough maturity to function independently. His body is developing rapidly, his muscles growing stronger. If all goes well, his horizon widens from month to month as new experiences pour in. He is, or should be, rapidly gaining independence, that is, the ability to make his own decisions and live without the supporting prop of his parents.

We, on the other hand, find our physical strength diminishing, our muscles and sense organs weakening. And worse, from having been the strong, supporting force in the family all during our mid-years, we are very apt to find ourselves becoming dependent in various ways, even if not financially. As the years go on, health and other problems will almost certainly force us to depend on others for many services. This can be galling, especially if we do not feel genuine affection in those who serve us. In any case, even under the best of circumstances, such as when those upon whom we must depend obviously respect and love us, the new situation is a severe comedown. Literally, old age is the only period of life when a loss of role does not almost automatically usher one into a new role. In American life old age is a time without a future. If we try to cling to the roles we had, we become nuisances and society is not slow to let us know it.

In old age we have not only to create our own new roles (and not just any old roles, but roles that allow us to feel useful and interested) but to create a set of values that in some ways go against the grain of general American values.

If we can't create those roles and values, we are lost. A great many of us are lost. The elderly psychiatrist, Olga Knopf, declares: "I am convinced that no old person is entirely free from at least occasional depressions." Depression in old age differs from that in youth in one respect, however. In the aged, the anger is directed more against himself than against anyone in the outer world. This selfhatred and self-rejection explain in part the high rate of suicide among the older generation."[2] (Suicide is the ninth highest cause of death among the old. This figure does not, of course, include the deaths euphemistically covered by the family by some such phrase as "died in his sleep.")

To experience changes like this, over however many years, is to experience an "identity crisis." One of its most exasperating features is that, like the earlier crisis, it is very hard to pin down in one's mind exactly where one is at the moment. Am I old or am I not? (Am I grown up or am I not?) What is expected

2. Olga Knopf, M.D., Successful Aging (New York: The Viking Press), p.22.

of me? (What am I supposed to be doing in this new period of my life?) If, as seems clear, many of my age group are not much approved of, how do I set about winning approval? (Do I say, "To heck with them all"?) How can I live on good terms with myself and with a society that has grave misgivings about the value of most people my age? All this when I'm not yet even sure that I'm old!

The folk wisdom is not much help. There was a time, I think, when old people more or less knew how they were expected to behave.

But now, about the best the folk wisdom can do is to wheel out some old saws, such as: "You're as old as you feel," or "Some people are older at forty than others at seventy." Much help such platitudes offer a sixty-year-old trying to place himself!

Remembering what his sixteen-year-old self felt about sexagenarians, he likely devotes some time on or around his sixtieth birthday to examining himself for signs of decrepitude. (At least I did.) What he probably finds is that he "feels" no different than he did at fifty. Indeed, he may even "feel" considerably better, because he has finished with many of the responsibilities that then weighed him down. So, temporarily, he relaxes, assuring himself that of course he will be old sometime, but the time is certainly not yet. Meanwhile, he will just not concern himself too much with what he sees in the mirror.

Joan Walsh Angland has said, "My mind never tells me – only the mirror speaks of the passing years." Very nice. But the fact is that most of us get to be quite clever at dealing with that mirror. Smiling at it, we find, will wipe off several years because the lines then run up instead of down. Or we may discover with one of my sisters that leaving off one's glasses also helps.

For obvious reasons the next climacteric comes at or around sixty-five, when most of us who are employed are pitched suddenly, with a more or less hypocritical ceremony of compliments and gifting, into retirement. Once more the aging person is apt to run a check upon himself.

"Maybe I've slowed down a bit since sixty," he may conclude. "My hair is certainly thinner and grayer. I may get tired a little quicker and my blood pressure has come up a bit. My near memory occasionally plays a bad trick on me by failing to come up instantly with correct information. But I'm still functioning pretty much as I always did. And I certainly don't feel old."

Nowadays, if we are lucky, we may in fact not be really old before seventy or, in favored cases, seventy-five or even later. Indeed, one prominent scientist in the field of aging, Dr. James E. Birren, has set up a table of life-span phases with eight divisions instead of the customary five. The table, he says, "takes into account not only the phases used by social institutions, but also psychological capacities, always recognizing that there are differences in age in individuals of the same age."[3]

Infancy	0-2
Preschool	2-5
Childhood	5-12
Adolescence	12-17
Early maturity	17-25
Maturity	25-50
Later maturity	50-75
Old age	75 –

Even if the table is realistic for only those individuals most favored in health, income, and interests, it throws a new light on what is now possible for those of us who are lucky in our life circumstances.

As many a senior has learned while puttering in his garden or roaming around the country in his camper or treating himself to a long-dreamed trip to Europe, the first years of retirement may actually be the happiest period in his life. For those of us who inherited

3. James E. Birren, The Psychology of Aging (Englewood Cliffs: Prentice-Hall, 1964), p. 5.

good bodies and treated them sensibly, and who also have many interests, reasonably sound emotions and an adequate income (how the "if's" mount up!), real old age now comes years later than it did in, say, 1920.

But at some time around seventy or seventy-five, even the lucky of us are forced to begin running through our surprised minds the astounding thought: "It has happened. I am old." We have known all along that time was sliding by and that eventually, if we managed to avoid death, we would be old. But the time was always somewhere in the misty future. How can it possibly be now? No matter how well we think we have prepared ourselves for old age, it is almost sure to come as the surprise described in the couplet by an unknown author:

"I have always known that at last I
   would take that road,
But yesterday I did not know that it
   would be today."

What finally convinces us is not so much the candles our children tactfully leave off our birthday cakes or the shock in the eyes of an old friend who has not seen us for several years as it is in the evidence within ourselves. We suddenly observe that the muscles in an arm have gone stringy. Or that we have unconsciously begun to sit or lean against something when putting on slacks. Or that clothing that once fit perfectly is now fitting badly. Or that a finger has begun to quiver uncontrollably. Or that our digestion has become so cranky that some foods must be forgone and none of them seems to have much flavor anymore. Or that our eyes or ears are markedly duller than they were only a few years ago, and that chores we were doing without thinking are now tiring.

Worse, oh much worse, the names of people and places are evading us. Suddenly, in the very middle of a sentence or an introduction of someone we've known for years, a word or a name is gone. **Eventually we remember it, but the experience is a little frightening as well as very embarrassing.** These are the events that let us know.

But the recognition is badly complicated by the fact that while the symptoms of age are being perceived, the "I" that sits behind every face feels itself to be just what it has always been. So it cannot really believe that what is appearing in the mirror or in the embarrassing memory lapses can be itself. Because the perpetually watchful "I" is incredulous, the person in the process of being brought to concede that he has become old has a real psychological problem on his hands. Like the little old woman who lost her petticoat, one is shocked by the primal question of identity: "Can this really be I?"

The problem is compounded by two facts of elderly life today: one, that the crisis is usually met in solitude; the other, that the general attitude of American society toward its old is one of profound disrespect.

What is needed, of course, is what has come to be called "consciousness raising." But who is around to help us with it? Within the last few decades there has evolved a whole professional class of counselors for the young. Also marriage counselors and vocational counselors and psychiatrists and "mind expanders" of assorted denominations, all dealing with the young and the middle-aged. But outside a handful of psychiatrists specializing in the problems of the elderly and a few overworked geriatricians (most of whom are barely middle-aged, so new is this medical speciality), who is around to help us with our special problems of identity? A well-married old couple who long ago learned to communicate their deepest feelings can greatly help each other, but many if not most old couples have never learned to enter the needed level of communication. And besides, there are all of the elderly singles – expecially us widows, who in our younger days were actively discouraged from talking too freely about our deepest feelings.

So most of us going into the stage of life known as old-age must do it alone and without much understanding or support. We don't even talk about it much among ourselves. Such talk as we have usually takes the form of wry jokes like, "I'm in the metallic stage, gold in my teeth, silver in my hair, and lead in my feet." Or the corny old, "My get-up-and-go has got-up-and-went."

Occasionally, when the arthritis gets too bad or money too scarce, we may let go and moan about our condition – whereupon everyone who decently can makes a quick departure from our presence, and we have had another good lesson in not talking about the problems.

As for sitting down to discuss seriously among ourselves the bewildering and overwhelming fact of having become old and of death waiting who knows how close, we just don't do it. Or at least we are only beginning to do it in some of the better senior citizen centers. It's as if we ourselves subscribe to the general notion that there is something improper about the subject. In such reticence, we tend to accept the general myths about us, one of which is that we are all alike and, therefore, all of us are helpless and need protection. Other myths are that we are demanding and set in our ways, lonely because we are not living with our families, on our way to an institution if not already there, and sooner or later going to become senile.

One of the first things I learned when I began to attempt real communication with old people about what was happening to us was how socially difficult my project was – even with people whom I knew very well. Once, for instance, when I playfully remarked to a brother-in-law that when I looked into a mirror I had the feeling that someone had played a bad joke on me, he exploded bitterly, "It makes me mad!" I was shocked by the real emotion in his voice, for I had always considered him a person practically imperturbable. Was his a common reaction, kept politely bottled except in moments of truth such as I had precipitated? Who knows? What I do know is that I quickly changed the subject.

The best literary statement I have seen of this phase of the identity problem of the old is another quotation by Beauvoir from Gide's Journal, which is to say, from the most solitary of writing, the journal of a professional writer:

If I did not keep telling myself my age over and over again, I am sure I should scarcely be aware of it. Nevertheless, even by repeating, "I am over sixty-five" like a lesson to be learnt by heart I can hardly persuade myself of it: all I manage to do is to convince myself of this – that the space in which my desires and my delights, my powers and my will can still hope to spread out is very narrow.[4]

4. Simone de Beauvoir, The Coming of Age (New York: G. P. Putnam's Sons, 1972), p. 295.

Or again, in words that have the ring of personal experience to many a senior not sufficiently gifted with words or self-analysis to have written them for himself:

My heart has remained so young that I have the continual feeling of playing a part, the part of the seventy-year-old that I certainly am; and the infirmities and weaknesses that remind me of my age act like a prompter, remind me of my lines when I tend to stray. Then, like the good actor I should like to be, I go back into my role and I pride myself on playing it."[5]

Beauvoir comments: "Was it true that he was consciously playing the character that society required of him? Or was it out of horror of old age that he looked upon his behavior as a seventy-year-old in the light of an act? At all events this passage once more emphasizes "the

5. Ibid.

unrealizable nature of old age."[6] (Italics mine.) How true! Only by taking careful note of the physical and mental changes that are happening in us can we realize that the time is finally now.

The other tangle of facts making the acceptance of one's having become old (that is, identifying oneself as one of the old) very difficult is the attitude of our culture toward its old. To return to Erikson's definition, the second part of identity formation consists of the individual's judging himself "in the light of what he perceives to be the way others judge him in comparison to themselves and to a typology significant to them."[7]

If the first phase of identifying oneself as old was subjective and hazy, this one is brutally clear. In a culture whose basic value is productivity, we are first pushed out of employment and then either judged useless or tolerated for our sentimental value. Though perhaps not as

6. Ibid., p. 296.
7. Erik H. Erikson, Identity, Youth and Crisis, p. 22.

completely as it was two decades ago, social esteem still largely depends on productivity. Today, as always, he who does not produce is felt to be a weight to be borne, gracefully or grudgingly, by society.

Particularly for those who come to it without financial reserves, old age can be a time of great cruelty. And never let it be forgotten that around 5,000,000 (or a good fourth) of us are below the poverty line. Just as the Eskimo grandmother, left to freeze in her igloo, was a side effect of her culture, these millions of old people are at least partly a side effect of our culture. They are the end result of a lifetime of lacks: too little money, too little education, too few stimulating jobs and experiences, inadequate diet and medical care, limited interests, and limiting emotions. If some of them are cantankerous or senile, who knows what they might have been under less grinding circumstances? The wonder is that so many have made of themselves interesting, lovable human beings in spite of all the limitations they met.

For these seniors the battle for self-respect must be really grim. Every colloquial term applied to them is disrespectful: "old coot," "geezer", "codger," "old crock," "grannies," "biddies", and "little old woman in tennis shoes," are only some of the common tags. (I could list a dozen more.) Even what was coined as a euphemism, "senior citizen," has acquired a comic connotation. In short, they are disrespected, given just enough income and medical attention to keep them alive – and are kept out of sight and out of mind as much as possible.

When people say, "Old age is so pathetic," they are usually thinking of the elderly sick and poor. We need to remember, however, that there are many kinds of old people in this country. Many are "comfortably situated." A few are rich, and they as well as the poor have special problems. (Suspicion, for instance, that people are drawn to them only because of their money and that everybody is scheming to get it.) A Florida psychiatrist has remarked about some of her patients who were buying $100,000 condominiums, "Unless the people in those buildings can find ways to get really involved with other people, those buildings might as well be called pre-burial vaults."

So far as cultural attitudes go, the plight of the elderly poor and lonely differs only in degree from that of the not-poor and not-lonely. The tiny percentage of old people who have won fame or general applause through a sizable contribution to the common good does not, of course, have this problem of social disrespect. 'What they may get is a somewhat patronizing celebration of what they were.)But for all the rest of us the attitude of our society toward the old is one of the hard facts we must confront in forming our new self-identification, our sense of "I am" and "I have a right to be." In his poem Provide, Provide, **Robert Frost** said it for all time:

No memory of having starred
Atones for later disregard,
Or keeps the end from being hard.[8]

To return to Erikson again:

An optimal sense of identity, on the other hand, is experienced merely as a sense of psycho-social well-being. Its most obvious concomitants are a feeling of being at home in one's body, a sense of "knowing where one is going," and an inner assuredness of anticipated recognition from those who count.[9]

Nothing I ever read or heard spoken more completely sums up the difficulties we face in thinking, "I've grown old." How can one "feel at home" in a body that every week and every year changes for the worse? And how can one

8. Robert Frost, Complete Poems (New York: Holt, Rinehart and Winston, 1964), p. 404.
9. Erik H. Erikson, Identity, Youth and Crisis, pp. 22-23.

have a sense of "knowing where one is going" when, if there is anything certain to the elder, it is that he can't know where he will be or in what "shape" he will be in a year or a decade hence – or even if he will be at all. And how can he feel assured of recognition when every year those who "count" for him personally dwindle in number and finally become so few that he feels almost denuded?

Any way one looks at it, the process of identifying oneself as old is not easy. No wonder our ambition tends to be to "stay young" rather than to become the best possible old person. To become the "best possible" elder is a very difficult, highly creative undertaking and should be so regarded by both the old person and those around him.

4

The Battle for Self-Respect

Even if we do fairly well at establishing a sense of "I" in a body utterly different from the one inhabited in earlier periods and even if we are lucky enough to be able to feel that we are pretty well set for an old age that will be at least tolerable, we run into another basic problem: We must like and respect the self we keep on discovering. And that, my dear juniors, is not easy in the time and place of today.

Perhaps it was never easy. In the second century Marcus Aurelius felt he had to admonish himself: "Never esteem anything as of advantage to thee that shall make thee break thy word or lose they self-respect." (Italics mine.' Note that he said "anything." Not riches, not power or affectionate companionship – not anything.

In our century T. S. Eliot laid bare much the same urgency in The Cocktail Party:

Half the harm that is done in this
    world
Is due to people who want to feel
    important
They don't mean to do harm – but
    the harm doesn't interest them,
Or they do not see it, or they justify it
Because they are absorbed in the
    endless struggle
To think well of themselves.

That "endless struggle" is an especially hard project for the old in a society that tends to push them aside as carelessly as it throws away beer cans. We, like everybody else, are affected by the feedback about ourselves that we are continually getting from others. To return again to the Erikson thesis about how identity is built, we are always caught in the interplay between what we like to think of ourselves and what we perceive to be the way in which others think of us. We can make a stout effort to be content with acceptance by "those who count for us personally," but it's not easy – especially in the later stages of old age, when many of those who "count" have passed on. Constantly reading disrespect in the eyes or the manner of those with whom we come into casual contact sets up a continual, abrasive self-questioning. Even if the attitude by the public for the old, we are put back to the "endless struggle to think well of ourselves." Hence, every time some salesman says to me, "And what can I do for you, young lady?" I am absolutely furious. Does he think me so stupid as to be flattered by that?

Tell us often enough by tone or manner that we are hasbeens not worth listening to respectfully, and presently we begin to believe it – or at least to wonder if it's not true. But if we are to live decent human lives we must some-how manage to preserve our self-respect. Or if, as often happens, we never really had much of it, we must try to create some at this late stage of life. We, like everybody else, need to like ourselves.

And what's more difficult, we have to keep on creating self-esteem. It's nothing we do once and can then forever after rest on our oars. If and when one of us decides he doesn't need to keep on growing in skill and knowledge and from here on out will just loaf about the house, his self-esteem begins to evaporate – and he begins in his own mind to be "just another old man or old woman." This fact he will also read in everybody's eyes and manner, thus hastening the process.

Because of the particular moment in history it was born into, my generation is especially vulnerable to the feedback it gets from others. For most of us there were always a good many obstacles in the way of our thinking well of ourselves. In our childhood, who concerned himself about our having a good self-image? The ministers and priests under whose watchful eyes we and our parents grew up (and their parents right on back for a very long time) worried not a minute about our having good self-images. Quite the contrary. The hymns of the period marveled that the crucifixion could purchase grace for "such a worm as I." (Not even a dog – just a worm!) Man was a sinner, "weak and vile." No health or goodness in him except as bought by the death of the Crucified.

When our parents accepted that as the human state, naturally they sought to scotch in us any little sign of sprouting conceit. Was not "pride" one of the seven deadlies? So, when we were children, the ultimate insult that we could fling at each other on the playground was "big-headed," meaning "conceited." Indeed today's pressure by child psychologists upon parents to try to build up self-esteem in children is quite new. Even yet, I seem to observe that most parents of young children tell them far more about their shortcomings than about their virtues. B. F. Skinner's "operant conditioning" by rewarding desired behavior instead of relying on punishment is still a long way from general family use. For us, growing up when the century was young, it was practically unheard of, though my parents did more of it than most.

Perhaps at this point we should try to clear up some of the confusion that befogs the terms "self-respect," "self-esteem," and "self-image." In dealing with any of them one does not go far without bumping into the fact that somewhere back in the history of the English language the now preferred term, "self-esteem," got mixed up with a lot of undesirable qualities, such as pride, conceit, egotism, and vanity. In one line the Random House Dictionary defines it as meaning "an objective respect for or favorable impres sion of oneself." But in the very next line it is an "inordinately or exaggeratedly favorable impression of oneself." The Webster definition is more flat-footed. For it, "self-esteem" may be either "self-respect" or "self-conceit." Because of this ambivalence we shall mostly be sticking to the older term, "self-respect," with the understanding that it means the right kind of self-esteem. But even "self-respect" is a somewhat slippery term, with the line between it and conceit often very thin. Who has not known the tall-talker who felt he was according himself only his proper due when everybody around him thought him grossly egotistic?

Today's psychologists talk about the self-image a great deal, believing that a realistic but favorable picture of oneself is essential to a successful life; that without this favorable picture, the individual is likely never to reach his potential either in productivity or personal growth. They also say flatly that, unlike intelligence or special gifts (as for music), it has nothing to do with inheritance. It is built up, most of them think, by the individual's experiences, starting from his earliest moments in his mother's arms and continuing on throughout lifetime interactions with other people.

Without a good self-picture and a decent amount of self-respect, they say, one believes oneself too clumsy or too stupid to succeed in one's undertakings, and therefore either tries halfheartedly or antagonizes people by overtrying. Or lacks the self-confidence to take risks by launching out into new experiences – and is therefore unnecessarily limited and rigid. Or feels so guilty over past misdeeds as to make quite impossible an acceptance of himself "warts and all." (I am oversimplifying, but it is important at this point to get some grasp of what is now thought to be the consequence of a favorable or negative picture of oneself.)

If the psychologists are right, anybody could predict that today's old people would find self-respect or esteem a particularly hard prize to come by. Our parents were Victorians, who passed on to us consciences now felt by the young and middle-aged to be overtender in some areas and insufficiently tender in others. Never let it be forgotten that one of us born in 1901 came into the world just as Victoria was leaving it. He was only thirteen when World War I broke out in Europe, barely through adolescence when it closed. He was, therefore, nurtured by parents who were fully Victorian, with a code of manners and morals that today seem almost to belong to the Middle Ages. The "refined" woman of that day would have fainted in her tracks at some of the language in today's novels and living rooms, at the explicitness of today's PG movies, or at the usual apparel on today's beaches.

Because our parents were Victorian or at least the product of Victorian manners and morals, most of my generation were taught: (a) that laziness was a sin – but we all knew in our hearts that we were badly tarred with that brush; (b) that disobedience was also sinful – but most of us were well aware that we obeyed only when the parental eye was upon us or when the rewards of disobedience did not promise to be very high; (c) that lying was a sin – but most of us knew well that we quite often took liberties with the truth; (d) that any form of sexual inquiry was a social blunder and any form of sex play a sin – but by hook or by crook most of us acquired information and experimented to some degree.

We were also told on numerous occasions that we were too noisy, or too cocky, headstrong, careless, irresponsible, wasteful, disrespectful, quarrelsome, and a long list of other reprehensible qualities. On the other hand, praising a child was thought to be a risky business. Hence, most of us did not hear much about it when we managed to comport ourselves well. The general parental rule-of-thumb was still the ancient, "Spare the rod and spoil the child." All of which practically guaranteed that later on we would run into problems with self-esteem. The teachers didn't help much either, particularly with the children who could not fit easily into the school program.

Small wonder that during all our lives most of us not only carried around a nagging sense of guilt but also had trouble knowing how to think and feel about ourselves. The wonder is that by early middle age most of us had shaken down to some kind of self-image we could live with.

After all, weren't we then producing the world's next crop of children? And bringing them up to the best of our ability? And acquiring skills needed by society? And managing somehow to get through all the wars and the Great Depression? And standing up to the stresses of the assembly line, business hierarchy, or professional life? In short, weren't we doing the world's work? (Remember, we were brought up on the "work ethic.") For our work, at least, we could respect ourselves because the whole of our society respected us for it. If we failed to "succeed" as we had once hoped we might, at least we were doing our share of work.

But along came the sixty-fifth birthday and we were no longer doing that work. The children were long gone to families of their own. The job, on which so much of our self-respect was based, had been taken from us. Worst of all, in this day of swiftly changing technical processes, the skills that were one of our chief bases for self-respect, may have become outmoded. In a very real sense they too have abandoned us. And along with them are going some of the more personal skills on which today's daily living depends, such as the ability to pilot a car easily in heavy city traffic.

Retirement, we need to remember, is a rather new phenomenon in this country. Until 1936, when the age for beginning to draw Social Security payments was set at 65 for men and 62 for women, people worked until they died or could no longer stand the stress of farm, factory, shop, or schoolroom. The Depression was still on at the time, and the urgent need to make room for younger people to enter the labor market was widely felt. So "retirement" quickly became a social institution, although its coming was delayed for a bit by the war-time needs for labor.

But as soon as the war was over and the first mass of backed-up demand had been met, 65 quickly became "the cut-off year." In all sorts of work places. Teachers who may or may not have become less efficient were put firmly out to grass, whereas formerly they might have hung on until general complaints forced them out. Assembly line workers and executives were also out, along with almost everybody else who worked for salary or wages.

When Social Security came into being, my generation was in its thirties. At the same time, in the mid-thirties, came the first antibiotics and many other new medical tools. Hence we are the first – the very first – generation not only to live longer but to have to deal with retire-ment-at-65 no matter what our physical or mental condition at that birthday. For this reason, we are, in a real sense, pioneers in the new American problem of how to live happily and usefully after retirement.

So here we are with a whole new life situation on our hands and with just as much need to "think well of ourselves" as we ever had, but the old bases for it gone. In this predicament we have two choices: Either we go back to the past and attempt to live on the bases it afforded or we try to find some new ones. If we take the first (and easier) way, we are soon judged to be "old fogies living in the past" and are accorded still less respectful attention by others. If we try the latter way, we come smack against the fundamental fact about self-respect: It must be created by the individual himself, but it largely depends on what he thinks or feels other people think or feel about him.

When I have questioned old people about their grounds for feeling good about themselves, I've found most of them making one or more of the following responses. "My children have turned out well" – meaning, "I brought them up well and now they do me credit." "I have lots of friends" – meaning, "I must be a fairly good person or I wouldn't have them." "I was a steady worker and saved my money and so accumulated enough to give me indipendence in my old age" – meaning, "The people I worked with or under recognized my worth and kept me on, and now I'm respected because I'm financially comfortable." "I have a place in the community" – meaning, "My church or other groups accept me and consider me worthwhile." "I'm still useful to quite a number of people" – meaning, "I am still needed." (They don't use sociologists' term "social role," but that is what they mean."

In the case of each of these commonly held grounds for the oldster's self-esteem, the respect accorded him by others is a basic ingredient. On the other hand, an elder bewailing his fate is almost sure to say (everybody has heard him) some, or all, of the following: "My children don't need me anymore" "I'm of no real use to anyone now." "I'm out of things – a has-been." "Nobody gives a rap for me or my ideas."

The word that describes that state of mind is "alienation." In the past decade sociologists and psychiatrists have been sounding alarms about the alienation of the minorities and the young. Because we seniors don't go in for drugs, don't often run afoul of the law, don't flaunt our outsiderness with outlandish hair and clothing styles, the word has not been applied to us. But if alienation is a feeling of being powerless, useless, and isolated, then a good many of us are in fact alienated. Many of us do feel estranged and excluded.

In one of the many studies of alienation completed in recent years Doctors Vern Bengston and William Martin worked out tests to measure the degree of alienation of the young, the middle-aged, and the old. Not surprisingly, the youth generation came up with the highest score – 84. But the old, the grandparental generation, also had a high score – 76. Both groups felt more powerless and meaningless than the middle or parent group.

In a society like ours, old age almost inevitably means loss of status – a severe blow to the ego. And the decreased income is only part of that loss. A retired colonel of my acquaintance summed it up admirably: "When I spoke, everybody around me jumped to action. Now there's only my family, and they don't jump." A military officer may have a more severe status problem than most of us face. But most of us are affected by it. Many newly retired executives or administrators, for instance, have to learn to answer a ringing telephone, so thoroughly accustomed are they to waiting for the secretary to act.

For most people in most occupations, retirement does in fact mean a drop in status. As an appellate judge put it, "If I retire, I'll be just another old man." He would still have his mind, his knowledge of the law, his wife, and a good income, but he would feel like "just another old man."

But the status loss is not the worst of it. Many old people feel deeply that they are no longer of any real use to anybody or anything. The old avenues of usefulness have closed off, and they do not know how to go about finding new ones. A sense of being worthless, of having no role, is the largest ingredient in the makeup of the unhappy, complaining old person whom everybody avoids as much as possible. It undercuts his sense of personal value at its most vulnerable point.

To this asault he may respond positively by seeking out new ways to be useful. Or he may develop more or less ingenious negative ways. He may, for instance, find occasions for bragging about his past achievements. Or he may turn sour and nastily downgrade the performance of acquaintances who are still in harness or who go out to do volunteer work. Or he may work hard at getting to be the "best doggone shuffle-boarder in town." Or he may just give up. In a society that considers him unimportant, and that thinks his only need is for money, it is very hard for him not to feel like a nothing.

Those of us lucky enough to have both a sturdy respect for ourselves and the ability to slip easily into new interests and occupations can hardly imagine how utterly wretched the lack of self-esteem can make a person, how empty and meaningless life can seem without it. Some of the afflicted sink to the pathetic level of an old woman in a nursing home whom a friend of mine impulsively stopped to chat with. As my friend, who had come to visit someone else and had only paused briefly, prepared to leave, the woman caught her hand and said passionately, "Thank you for seeing me." She had come to feel herself so worthless as to be invisible.

Almost anybody who goes to call in nursing homes can duplicate the pathos of this story. In her book, Nobody Ever Died of Old Age, **Sharon Curtin concludes that in some "homes" the sense of having lost all claim for respect is actually fostered by the institution's staff, because then all the old people can be treated in one impersonal way. In other words, depersonalization, the deprivation of all claim for respect, makes for easier care.**

The nursing home situation is, however, only the extreme. People still thoroughly mobile and with reasonably good incomes react badly to feeling useless. Some become ill-tempered or querulous. Others grow contentious or, if they always had a tendency to over-value money, become greedy and tight-fisted. Still others hungrily bid for praise and then repeat over and over whatever compliments they have been able to cadge, until their acquaintances are either much amused or much annoyed.

But why go on listing the unfortunate responses we make to feeling useless, to having no role. Everybody who has dealt

with old people can make a good list of his own. Somehow this society has to do something about its alienated old people as well as its alienated youth and minorities.

And just giving us more money won't be enough. Rene Duclos said it well in The God Within.[1]

The need for direct participation in the affairs of the group is another aspect of human life that is universal, probably because it has roots deep in the biological past. To a very large percentage of people, perhaps to all, this need is more intense than the thirst for knowledge or respect for pure reason. Man is a social animal in a deep biological sense.

Society does need to mend its ways with us. The culture is against us much as the Eskimo culture was against the grandmother who had become a weight

1. Rene Duclos, The God Within, p. 191.

the group could not carry. Not as piti-
lessly, of course, for our elders are given
enough social security payments to keep
them alive, and many individuals are
kind and understanding. But no one in
his senses doubts that our struggle for
self-respect is unnecessarily harsh
because of the general attitudes and
customs.

Consider Cicero's famous remark:
"Old age, especially honored old age, has
so great authority that it is of more value
than all the pleasures of youth." Even
though one knows that he was speaking
of the elders in the Roman upper class to
which he belonged, the words today
sound like self-serving rhetoric. If it
really was true of his class in his point of
history, it certainly isn't true now. How
many old people now have "authority?"
A handful of outstanding professional
people, a few very successful writers and
artists, a few officials who have managed
to continue getting themselves reelected,
and a diminishing number of men who
own their own businesses and have not

yet been shoved aside by younger members of the family or gobbled up by a conglomerate. Altogether a tiny percentage of our many millions.

At times, however, when I have listened to old people discuss their grievances, I have had the heretical thought that they have too easily assumed that the ability to feel good about oneself and one's life is something handed out by God and/or the Great Mother, society. Hence, we either have it if they are generous with us or we don't have it if they are stingy.

This latter attitude, remember, is the exact conclusion reached by Simone de Beauvoir in the passage already quoted: "It is the fault of society that the decline of old age begins too early, that it is too rapid, physically painful, and because entered in upon with empty hands, morally atrocious." It's all the fault of society, she says flatly, with nothing or almost nothing that the individual can do about it. Either we've been handed a life-situation in which we can feel good about ourselves or we haven't. We can organize to bring pressure for better social security rates. But how could we organize to acquire more self-respect and more social respect? What set of politicians could be lobbied for that?

Much of what is now being said and written about the problems of the old agrees with the Beauvoir position. In some of the stories of isolated, poverty-ridden, sick old people, one gets the feeling that the feature writers wholly agree with Beauvoir that the old have been completely victimized by society; they seem to agree that the individual is helpless, in fact has been helpless all his life unless he happens to have belonged to "a handful of privileged people."

On the other hand, we hear Pearl Buck saying just as flatly that we can only be respected by others if we respect ourselves. "Respect can only be won by the dignity of self-respect," said she in the last year of her life.

On the face of it there doesn't seem to be much possibility of reconciling these views of two of the world's most gifted women. But perhaps there is. In recent years we have been seeing that in our society, if a large minority considered by some to be inferior (and thus doomed to excessive difficulty with regard to self-respect) can get themselves together to understand that the supposed inferiority is not inherent but societal, a first step has been taken toward easier self-respect. When this has been done, a helpful slogan (Black is Beautiful) can be invented. In "consciousness raising groups" all over the country, rebellious women have been considering their position in society. When the cultural weighting is understood, individuals can at least begin to work at building up self-esteem.

The philosophers, and more recently the psychology popularizers, have always said that there is something we can do about our attitudes towards ourselves, even when the cultural attitudes are against us. We can, for instance, begin to do some real thinking about ourselves as minority members of a very large, very complex, in some ways very cruel society instead of just accepting the feedback of what our younger associates seem to be thinking about us.

Do they convey the impression, either by ignoring us or by ushering us too solicitously into the best chair in the room, that we are really no longer interesting, functioning human beings but creatures of a special order, to be either ignored or treated with exaggerated courtesy? Well, that is their problem. Ours is, first and always, to be interested and then to be conscious of the fact that we are interested, and then to share our interest with others. After that we take our chances on being thought interesting.

For another thing, the elder can do some hard thinking about himself. Does he feel guilty about something he may have done? He can stop nagging himself. We are all wrong-doers, and the chances are that he is no more odiously tarred than most of us. He can, yes he can, do whatever is possible to rectify whatever wrongs he has done to others, then forgive himself for the mistakes of the past and get on with the living of today. This, I well realize, is the preachiest of all prescriptions and one of the hardest to take, but it is also one that effective human beings in every culture and religion have been practicing for a very long time.

Does he feel resentment at some of the raw deals life has handed him? Nothing makes old age so empty and bitter as resentment over what happened and cannot now be undone. Some sessions of thinking and talking about what happened may clarify the grounds for resentment. In the perspective of time they may turn out to be less grim than we have been thinking. In any case, the session will help us to forgive and forget – and thus to get rid of some heavy baggage.

Or perhaps the elder is succumbing to the feedback, to what he takes to be the attitude of those around him that he is a useless, barely tolerated object taking up space and taxes and contributing little or nothing in return. If this is the real nub of his struggle for self-esteem, the answer to it was given by Max Ehrman nearly fifty years ago: "You are a child of the universe, no less than the trees and the stars; you have a right to be here." Christians say it differently, but mean much the same: "I deeply regret my mistakes and errors. But I am a child of God. By His grace I am forgiven and granted a right to respect myself."

It was, I suspect, learning how to conduct such sessions with herself that made Pearl Buck able to say confidently in her seventy-ninth year: "I am a far more valuable person today than I was 50 years ago, or 40 years, or 30, 20, or even 10. I have learned so much since I was 70! Indeed I can honestly say that I have learned more in the last 10 years than in any previous decade."

Then she went on in what was probably one of her last statements about the difficult business of learning how to live and how to continue learning right into the last years. "Year by year, we work for techniques in order to master ourselves and reach a growing understanding of ourselves and others. . . . We must understand ourselves before we can respect ourselves. We must respect ourselves before we can win the respect of others."

Of course it is much easier for someone with her achievements to feel herself continually growing in value than it is for Joe Jones or Mary Smith. But one has to be stirred when she says unabashedly, "Age deserves respect, but respect can be won only by the dignity of self-respect." "Learning to understand ourselves," she adds, "is the key to self-respect." That learning, I am finding, is a task not completed at fifty or even sixty-five. Or eighty. Unless or until our mind departs us completely, the task of self-understanding, basic to self-esteem, goes on as long as we are alive.

5

... And Assorted Other Battles

We used to be admonished about "growing old gracefully." Nowadays the phrase is "successful aging." Whatever the wording, the scientists and crusaders interested in us and our problems are pretty well agreed on the essentials for a "good" old age: sufficient income to provide an adequate diet, comfortable housing, and proper medical care (and then the wit and the will to make that income really provide those essentials); an active mind and some genuine interests; a feeling of being needed and useful; and a basic life-loving attitude.

Note that income is listed first. Our problems are much more than financial, but a certain amount of income is absolutely essential. As I have gone about asking elderly acquaintances and strangers what they relied on most to help them through this last stage of life, I have been interested to observe how many of them have listed income first. It seemed to fall automatically off most tongues. Even some people who have been religious all their lives spontaneously said, "enough income." As one of them summed it up, "If you have a comfortable income you can have the food, housing, and medical care you need for health. You can buy books and hobby materials. And you can afford transportation to take you out into the community."

In any case old age is very far from being the serene meadow that young or middle-aged writers used to picture it as being. It is a time of struggles and decisions not less harrowing than those of any other stage of life.

In at least one way, however, these struggles differ from those of earlier life: they are more hidden. Indeed, any reasonably bright old person knows that if he wants to retain the company of his juniors he had better keep the struggles hidden! Old people have a bad reputation for grumbling. During our time all of us have known seniors who complained themselves right into isolation. If we still have any sense at all, we know that if we talk much about our worries and pains, even our contemporaries will give us a wide berth and our children will see as little of us as their sense of duty permits. If we don't want to be isolated, we had better appear untroubled, even if what we really want to do is let forth a loud, clear gripe.

Being old means fighting a whole series of battles on a number of fronts, not all of them equally severe for all seniors and probably not all of them equally severe for any senior at various times in his life. But all of them are guaranteed to affect all of us in some ways and in some periods.

Before we begin to consider these battles, perhaps we should set up a distinction made by a gerontologist friend of mine, Dr. Dorothy Larsen. It is her observation that what is called "old age" is roughly divided into three parts.[1] There are, of course, no hard and fast timetables and no sharp dividing lines between them, because some people age faster than others both physically and mentally. And others contract a disease, such as cardiac trouble, that may carry them off suddenly and thus keep them from ever entering the final stages. But if the elder lives, all the periods emerge, she says, with fairly well-marked divisions between them. First, of course, is the period immediately following retirement, when the oldster may have so much energy that he can take on many new activities and keep up with them happily and without undue stress. Then comes what she calls "the frail" period – what Midwesterners used to call being "feeble." This is a time when he finds he must limit his activities, take only one appointment per day instead of going from early till late – when he "sits" more

1. Dorothy Larsen, Ed. D., Dialogs on Aging (Published by Teachers College Press, New York).

than he did earlier. At the very end comes the hopefully short period of "sleeping," when he is bedfast and perhaps either unconscious or almost so.

This rough charting of old age is something like the one most sensible parents make in dealing with their teenagers. Because puberty and early adolescence are not so very different from late childhood, they keep some of the rules and protections of the previous period. But the twelve-year-old is quite a different creature from the one he becomes in three more years. And by the time of late adolescence, he is still different. And woe to the parents who have failed to recognize the changes and to institute appropriate changes in their own behavior and their relationships with him as he moves from one stage to another.

In much the same way the newly retired, if he is lucky in his health and interests, may go ten years before beginning to flag perceptibly. An increasing number of old people seem to be staying longer in the first, active period, so that the time of being frail is shorter. Because of the new drugs and life-prolonging techniques, the terminal or "sleeping" period may be horribly extended – or by some good chance a heart attack may reduce this period to nothing. But whatever happens, we who are passing through the changes need to understand them and have them understood by those around us.

The battles will change as the ground shifts from the active, sometimes too active, time of early retirement to the enforced quietude of the last days or months. But battles they are and battles they will remain to the end of consciousness.

LIVING WITH THE BODY'S BETRAYAL

If betrayal seems too strong a word, it is a highly personal choice. The "I" that sits behind my shriveling face knows that there are just as many interesting places to see as there ever were and is just as eager to see them. It also knows that there are as many, indeed many more, interesting things to do than in, say, 1920 and that it would have a great time trying to do some of them. But my eighty-year-old body shudders away from the physical hardships of travel – the tension and red tape involved in presenting oneself to airlines at the right moment, the irregular hours, the extra walking, the strange foods and beds. I have, so "I" flatters me, still enough skills and experience to make a competent board member in one of "my" organizations. But my body reminds me of smoke-fogged meetings when my head will ache and of long sittings in meeting and before the telephone when another part of me will ache, of icy mornings when "I" shall feel it prudent to stay home, of the dulling ears that make group discussion a strain.

If these quavers from my body do not constitute betrayal of my "I", then I do not know what the word means. For people who have always been lively and ambitious this contest between their "I" and their body is one of the hard facts of old age. Sometimes the body is right. But sometimes it is just being lazy and needs to be prodded. Deciding when to accept and when to prod is one of the real struggles of old age, none the less real for being unseen by onlookers.

Old people have, of course, always had to contend with the body's "going back on" them. No doubt it has always been a shock for them to discover that they cannot safely undertake an activity that they once entered into almost without thought. But former generations of oldsters were not so numerous as we are. And they did not live so long. (Buckminster Fuller has been pointing out that when he was born his father's life expectancy was 27 and his own was 42.) There were, of course, the storied old pine knots who kept on practicing medicine or running their stores until well into their eighties and the rugged grandmas who continued to cook and garden until a like age. But they were the exceptions and became almost legendary in their neighborhoods.

Moreover, there was a kind of tradition about how to behave when old. One was expected to "sit by the fire" and if it was necessary, depend upon the children – or the County if the children could not manage. This latter was felt to be a fate worse than death, but it was there, part of the order of things. Altogether, there was a fairly clear and generally accepted pattern for how to act in old age. It may not have been a stimulating or pleasurable existence, but at least the old knew how they were expected to behave.

My paternal grandfather, for instance, sat in his daughter's home and read for the last fifteen of his eighty-six years. He went for a walk every day, to church every Sunday, and to the bank once a month to cash his Civil War pension check. Otherwise he sat in his room and read. The only useful function he served was entertaining the grandchildren by reading to them or telling them tales about the Civil War or pioneer life in Kansas. That was his life, he enjoyed it, and nobody expected it to be anything else. When he was eighty-six, he got erysipelas and was gone in three days. Today he would be given some antibiotics and sent home to resume his sitting.

There is now no generally accepted tradition for our behavior. How could there be? Social changes have poured in too fast for traditions to have formed. We are denied gainful employment, then felt to be nuisances because we sit around and complain. The two or three generation home is now something nobody wants, we least of all. "Retirement apartments" are sprouting everywhere, but living in one of them means acquiring what amounts to a whole new life-style for most old people, also being at least partly segregated from the rest of society. Our children move from one city to another, and old friends either move away or die off. All of which means that when the husband or wife is gone, we mostly have to fight the body's betrayal

110

by ourselves and without any firmly marked out path.

What is worse, no matter how much intelligence and spirit we are able to summon up for the battle, it is going to be lost – and knowing it is a loser does not make it easier for the body to fight. The aging body will give us an increasing burden of "aches and pains." Even if we are sufficiently lucky as to have so few of them that an occasional aspirin will comfort us, they are present – and guaranteed to get worse. We can and do become somewhat inured to them, but continual low-grade pain is a hard condition to live in – especially since it is very likely to become more than low-grade.

In addition, there are organ deteriorations to contend with. These happen to the best of us as well as to the stinkers. For instance, a friend of mine who was one of the nation's better known professors of government is at eighty-plus still a sharp observer of the current scene and would love to make what he knows available to his town and state. But his auditory nerves have failed so badly that even with the best hearing-aid on the market he can hardly function in a group.

Another friend was a good psychologist who could be doing research in his retirement. But he has Parkinson's Disease. His time and energy (and his wife's) are therefore consumed in a holding action against a disease that medical science is only beginning to be able to treat.

Another, a grandmother and beautiful spirit who has been an editor in a university press, can travel only with hypodermic dosages of folic acid in her purse and to homes where she can herself prepare her severely limited diet. Still another, who was an unusually good teacher and is still an accomplished raconteuse, has very high blood pressure and lives under constant threat of a stroke.

These four are picked almost at random from among my relatives and close friends. I could cite many more. And of course we are all more or less plagued by arthritis, and lucky if we don't also have either cataracts or glaucoma, diverticulosis or arteriosclerosis. Even without disease the organs wear out. Joseph P. Lash quoted Eleanor Roosevelt as saying, "Inevitably there are aches and pains, more and more, and if you pay much attention to them, the first thing you know you are an invalid."

A cousin of mine put it in more masculine terms in a letter describing his reaction to the cane his doctor had urged upon him as a possible relief for an arthritic hip:

It does seem to be true, damn it, that the cane relieves the pain to some small degree. But how do you carry packages to the post office? And where do you put the blasted thing when you're not using it? It doesn't fit anywhere in a car. Then another point: The aging psyche suffers so many blows to its dignity. You wear a wig or you're bald; you wear false teeth or you don't chew; you take a little white pill or your blood pressure goes up; the barber cuts more hair out of your nose and ears than off the top of your head; you begin to thicken inexplicably about the neck and waist; your memory is not as sharp as it once was.

Then a well-meaning doc comes along and says, "Let's try a cane," and the first thing you know you resent the thing. So I used it a week or so and have not used it since and have no intention of so doing.

In spite of all the medical advances, Seneca's sour comment that "old age is an incurable disease" still has a certain validity. The twentieth century increase in the average life span has been mostly due to getting control of many infectious diseases. Children need no longer die of diphtheria, scarlet fever, or "summer complaint," and an antibiotic will usually take care of acute infections in adults. What we die of now is chronic disease.

Dr. Josef P. Hrachovec of the Gerontology Center at the University of
Southern California has suggested that
the present average life span would be
extended by about ten years if medical
science were to discover how to prevent
or cure such diseases as heart trouble
and strokes. If and when cancer comes
under control, life expectancy would
move up another sizable notch, and so
on through the chronic diseases.

Looking at it anyway we want, there
does seem to be a real connection
between old age and disease. Seneca was
off base in thinking old age a disease in
itself, but it is certainly linked with the
presence or absence of disease – and is
itself, no matter how far the scientists learn to extend it, finally incurable.
No amount of medical advance or personal "spirit" can wholly prevent the
body's betrayal. We are mortal.

Another result of the aches-and-pains
and organ deterioration syndrome may
be difficulty in finding a doctor. Many
doctors don't like taking on old patients

(some M.D.'s refer to us as "old crocks") because we never really get well. Geriatrics is such a new specialty that it has few practitioners. Perhaps it will never have many, because specialties are chosen when doctors are young, and because doctors like to see their patients get well. About the most they can hope to do for us is to make us more comfortable. Besides, old people don't always obey instructions. They may not understand them. Or they may cut down on medications because they feel they can't afford them – or because they are just contrary.

As a class we are not popular in doctors' offices, and when we have to find a new doctor, it can be difficult to locate one with whom we can establish a relationship that includes respect on both sides.

MAINTAINING INTERESTS AND CREATING NEW ONES

Everybody who lifts pen or voice on the subject of aging zeroes in at once on the importance of having "interests." Most of the retirees who have looked forward to "plenty of rocking and fishing" are likely to get very bored with the chair and fishing rod. Not all, of course. Some will settle down happily to such a life – and not irritate their wives by attempting to horn in on the household management. But by and large, I suspect that this is the group that has given rise to all the wife-and-retired-husband jokes that presently abound in the land.

Enough studies have now been done to let us know for certain that the elders who maintain a lively interest in anything whatever are apt to cope well with the increasing disabilities of old age. From duplicate bridge to ward politics, from tracking down ancestors to writing an autobiography to let grandchildren or later descendants know "how it was," it has been statistically demonstrated that the elder who keeps plugging away at something that genuinely interests him has the best chance to retain health and vigor.

The trouble is that interest-cultivation must begin a long way before age sixty-five – the longer the better. If a retiring salesman, for instance, has been an enthusiastic gardener or Sunday painter or wood-carver for twenty years, he is practically guaranteed not to have any difficulty with his extra hours. But if his only real interest was in his job and spectator sports, he isn't very likely to start up hobbies or other compelling interests after retirement. And the woman whose life has been bounded by house and yard isn't a good prospect for either crafts or community work. Nearly all of those who tell themselves that "as soon as the children are gone" they will become active in community affairs are very unlikely to do it. If by the time they are fifty they haven't acquired a real interest in a social problem or a purposeful organization plus some group skills, they are going to feel so awkward and timid in groups that genuine interest and participation is practically impossible. I have seen such women, when asked to read a minor, typed-out report, suffer such agonies of fright that the paper in their hands rattled audibly or their knees quivered visibly. It's a rare person who will risk such stress and embarrassment a second time.

We may as well face it: The Archie and Edith Bunkers of the country are very rarely going to launch out into new activities. Archie will probably keep on with his bowling until arthritis rules him out. Edith will go on attending the women's group of her church or maybe rolling bandages for the Red Cross until these activities get to seem like too much effort – or Archie objects to her being out of the house so much. Both of them will be bored and boring.

This matter of "interest" is, of course, important for people of all ages, but it is absolutely crucial for the elderly. The aches and pains ensure that. As Mrs. Roosevelt said, if we haven't interests sufficiently compelling to take our minds off our increasing disabilities, the "first thing we know" we are invalids, or at least too "frail" to be out and doing.

Perhaps this is the place to start driving home my conviction, which will be elaborated later, that for most of us hobbies alone do not really fill the bill. They are helpful, but nothing takes the place of a sense of being useful in some, however small, way – a sense of having a role.

As American society is now organized, the old have no function – no role that another group cannot fill. The philosophers have always said that the old had an important social function: to transmit history and tradition. This cannot now be our function. For one thing, tradition itself has lost much of its force. Too many traditions have been wiped out in recent years. For another, the young now have far more exciting things to think about than the past. The Great Depression struggles of my generation are positively tedious beside the dramatic events chronicled on almost any newspaper's front page. And even if the grandchildren are disposed to listen, they are likely to be prevented by sheer distance. Many of us see our grandchildren only for a week or so out of the year, because their parents have been moving from one part of the country to another. Or, just as likely, we may have moved to a retirement center in some Southern state. In either case distance effectively rules most of us out of the tradition business.

If the molecular biologists succeed in "slowing down the time clock" and if at the same time the present trend toward earlier and earlier retirement continues, society is going to be compelled to do something about using its elderly. Some unions are now trying to get their companies to retire employees at fifty-five or "after thirty years" even if the worker came to the company at age eighteen. When so many jobs are either mind-dulling or back-breaking, one can understand why employees should want to leave them early. But an economy must be able to support its pensioners –

and that is an accomplishment ours has still to demonstrate over the long haul. Some economists are now warning that it won't be permanently able to support such a large population of pensioners in idleness – at least not without changing our whole national system of priorities. Meantime the pressures for earlier retirement go on. Consequently, all of us, of whatever age, had better begin to take this whole series of problems more seriously.

Within ten or twenty years, I predict it will have long since become apparent that millions of us cannot be and need not be supported in housebound soul-rotting idleness. A function, or at least the outline of one, will have had to be found for us, one for which some of us can be paid something, but which will not upset the orderly entrance of the young into the labor market. What the role will be, nobody now knows, but the best of my generation is already pioneering in such research. The Swiss psychiatrist Paul Tournier, has some suggestions that we shall be looking at in his last book, Learn to Grow Old.

During our long years we have developed skills useful not just for shop, assembly line, or other work place, but for living as human beings with other human beings. We can hunt for places to use those skills. Both the federal and some state governments have launched promising new programs for using these skills. With encouragement we ourselves might even develop some new skills! Meantime the acquisition of not only real interests but socially useful skills should be a basic part of our preparation for old age.

At present, however, the cards are stacked against the elders who were always "too busy" to take on positions of responsibility in community organizations. They will spend their later years puttering about the house or lounging before the television set. And they will end up tiresome and self-pitying.

But even those who already have some well established interests and skills will need a good measure of determination. Any personality flaw that in earlier years might have been overlooked for the sake of getting the group's work done is now so deeply embedded that it seriously handicaps us in a group. More than that, unless we have some real personal distinction, the very fact of our gray hair assigns us, at least at first, to such stimulating tasks as addressing envelopes and stapling together the newsletter sheets. We learn, if we disagree with a line of action our group is proposing, either to "go along" in silence or to present the disagreement in very tactful and tentative terms, because, being old, we are ipso facto supposed to be constitutionally opposed to change – an old geezer or a little old lady in tennis shoes.

To repeat once more, we see ourselves at least partly through other people's eyes or what we think they are seeing in us. What we feel they think of us tends to become part of our self-image. When we are commonly felt to be has-beens, we tend to accept that judgment, hence to be diffident, even somewhat apologetic in presenting our ideas or offering our services. Because the general impression is that old brains have inevitably deteriorated, we become self-conscious over memory lapses that once we would have laughed at.

I furnished myself a perfect lesson in such self-consciousness a few years ago when a luncheon committee meeting was sadly delayed by the lateness of a key member, a man in his middle forties.

He finally arrived, full of apologies and much merriment. "I have to catch planes so often," he chuckled, "that I forgot I was supposed to be here today and didn't remember until I got almost out to the airport."

"You know," confessed another middle-ager, "I did that very same thing not long ago."

As they enjoyed their memory failures, I regarded them with a vinegary mixture of wonder and animosity. If that had happened to me at my age, I knew in my soul, I would have suffered a wave of smothering dread as I thought, "I'm slipping!" And never, never, would I have confessed my blunder in public.

Perhaps what we most need on such occasions is to be reminded, as his wife reminded a man I know, "But, dear, you were always like this." We may not relish the reminder, particularly if it has the wifely or husbandly ring of one who never lost things or had trouble remembering what he was supposed to do next. But to be admonished that we had memory lapses back-when puts things in perspective, instead of turning them into fingerposts to senility.

The aphorism about old dogs and new tricks haunts us even if we proclaim that we don't accept it. Most of us are not aware of the recent studies that show that most old people can continue to learn, although at a somewhat slower pace. Even the dog books now concede that good old Fido can learn new tricks, although more slowly than when he was a pup.)

During the last fifteen years many studies have been made of mental losses in the old. One of the chief scientists in the field is Dr. James E. Birren, Executive Director of the Andrus Gerontology Center at U.C.L.A. In a long series of experiments with rats he and his students years ago learned that old rats are slower than young rats in their response to stimuli, also that in an experimental tank they swam more slowly. But in another experiment, when he reversed an already learned maze, Dr. Birren found that the old rats relearned as well as the young.

When the studies shifted to people, the same results showed up. The reaction time of older people was slower than that of young people. On an instrument that would show differences of one-hundredth of a second, 30 young adults were tested against 23 elderly people. The tests covered a variety of situations, such as reaction to a simple stimulus, to verbal tests such as word completions, choices, associations, and so on. Again the same result: The old reacted more slowly than the young. But they did learn, and as far as vocabulary scores were concerned, they scored higher than their juniors.

It should be noted that the muscular slowing observed in both rats and humans may in the latter be at least partly voluntary. As older people begin to sense loss of balance, they may train themselves to move more slowly in order to lessen the danger of falling. I watch myself doing this all the time. After a fall on the ice last winter, I shan't be out on the ice again except in real emergency. No longer do I scamper up and down stairways disregarding the handrails, and I am trying to train myself to a watchful respect for hazards in the footing just ahead. The voluntary slowing may also be partly in response to a warning from a relative or friend that I should begin to slow down. (All of us hear that!) At any rate and from whatever cause, moving more slowly and thinking more slowly do seem to be part of growing old.

Another significant Birren study checked the rate of mental loss in 47 healthy men with an average age of 72. This study, begun in 1963, was followed by another on the same men in 1968, to see what changes in their mental abilities had occurred in the five intervening years. Some of the men showed considerable deteriorations, others none whatever. This led Dr. Birren to conclude that a "subset" of patients who suffer from organic brain damage deteriorates mentally while others show little if any change. These results, he thought, suggest that the average person does not need to expect a "typical deterioration" in his mental abilities as he ages. "The expectation is that, given good health and freedom from cerebral vascular disease and senile dementia, individuals can expect mental competence to remain at a high level beyond the age of 80." (Emphasis mine.)

In a more recent study (1969) Dr. Birren found that older people have apparently "developed cognitive strategies that enable them to react quickly and efficiently in ways that young people do not know." This, he speculated, may be because they have "learned through experience what is important and what is surface."

Today's scientists in growing numbers are giving attention to the relationship of brain disease to senility and are increasingly convinced that the relationship need not be progressive, but with proper attention can be halted and the patient rehabilitated. One recent breakthrough is said to be a technique for discovering a clogged carotid artery, then reaming it out so that the brain can continue to be nourished. Rehabilitation procedures after "small strokes" are another important new way to ward off senility. As said earlier, some professionals are begining to believe that some of what is commonly called "senility" may really be chronic depression – and for that there are now drugs and other therapies. In the future, we shall probably be seeing a much lower percentage of "senility" than is now current.

More will be known. Meantime, we might begin to live with more exercise, less emotional tension, and decreased table salt, say the scientists.

What the studies show is that we are a very diverse group – fully as diverse as any other age grouping of humanity. Some of us are stupid, senile, and/or depressed. Others, those of us who have had a reasonably fair shake in life and have also managed to avoid the brain-damaging diseases, can retain our mental power. Agility and quickness of response we have probably lost and will continue to lose. Mental ability, maybe, but not necessarily. And the backs of our hands to everybody who thinks that just because we have turned sixty-five (or eighty), we must therefore be losing our marbles.

If the "interests" situation is already very troublesome for us, it is probably going to get even worse. If Dr. Hrachovec is correct in his prediction that a life expectancy of one hundred is altogether possible for the children now being born, this extension of life will greatly exacerbate the present social problems in finding a useful function for the post-retirement years. Does anybody seriously believe that people can be outside the work world for thirty-five years without consequences we can now only speculate about?

But a much more radical possibility that Dr. Hrachovec's is also being forecast as the result of a research program underway in the Veteran's Administration since 1963. According to a news report put out in May, 1973, preliminary findings seem to indicate that in the fairly near future the normal life expectancy might be extended to 120 or even to 140 years. (This preliminary report, interestingly enough, accords exactly with the extraordinary life spans achieved in three remote, mountainous areas of the world where many people live active, useful lives, until long past the century mark. The areas, which have been studied at first hand by Dr. Alexander Leaf of Harvard Medical School, are Abkhasia in the Caucasus region, Hunza near the border of China and Pakistan, and Vilcabamba, 11,595 feet up in the Andes Mountains of Ecuador.)

On top of the staggering problems we may expect if the preliminary reports of the V.A. study continue to be borne out as the study proceeds, the news release adds that the predicted extension of life expectancy "will be accompanied by a high degree of competency, with the result that people in their eighties will be much more active than at present." Who knows, perhaps the frolicsome eighties of the future will become as restive over their situation as the teen-agers of the 60s were! This whole society, and especially all of us seniors, had better begin to concern ourselves with finding useful, interesting outlets for the energies of the old. Those energies may be about to increase enormously.

Meantime, our purpose should be to stay healthy by means of a sensible program of diet, exercise, mental aliveness, and pursuit of activities that both appeal to us and allow us to maintain a social role. That program should, of course, properly have begun by at least age 45. But if it didn't, 65 or 75 is not too late to launch forth, although the late adventuring will probably take more fortitude and spunk than earlier. Much of our society, even sometimes our middle-aged children, would prefer that we sit quietly, partly because we are then less likely to become nuisances, and partly because quietness is safer. It is unfortunately true that we are less apt to break a bone while knitting or placidly watching TV than while transporting ourselves to some scene of interesting or useful activity. But it's hard, if not impossible, to get anything but boredom from a steady program of sitting. Because our own inclination may be to sit passively sheltered from the problems and stresses that will assault us the minute we strike out into new activities, the temptation may be to "sit" too soon and too much, instead of pushing ourselves out into new interests and then pouring ourselves enthusiastically into them.

But even when we have pushed and then let ourselves go into enthusiasm, there are difficulties, and not just those of the aches and pains variety. Those of us who are hard of hearing will not find group discussion easy, even when we are properly fitted with a good hearing aid – a thing harder to come by than many unwary oldsters suppose. The eyes may no longer tolerate long bouts of reading. Stiffening hands impede music making, typing, or crafts. Even sleeping is likely to become a problem and waking up to be a tussle with leg cramps and balky joints.

In the face of all this, the old people who remain genuinely interested in the business of living and determined to make some kind of contribution to the common life – and a host of such do exist – deserve medals for a very special kind of valor and achievement.

"DISENGAGING" WISELY

One of the disagreements among gerontologists and others who study or deal with old people concerns activity and disengagement. Nobody doubts that old age is a time of "disengagement," or as I prefer to refer to my decisions of that sort, "withdrawals." The question is, how soon and how fast? Should the elder push himself to remain active as long as he possibly can or should he let go when he is still relatively strong and active? I know that it is an article of faith among the old and their partisans to bewail the injustice of forced retirement, but I confess to some ambivalence about the imposition of a set retirement age. One can freely admit that it is not only unjust but stupid of society to put all workers out to grass at age sixty-five, but there is another side to the problem. For some people in some jobs, sixty-five may be too young. But for others it may be too old. In either case the problems of personnel administration in even a fair-sized organization would be much more difficult. Nor would the individual worker be without problems. Even if physical and mental examinations could definitely determine which workers were still fully fit to go on working and for how long, those who were let go might always have to carry a load of resentment and a feeling of favoritism. And so long as the rate of unemployment among the young is as high as at present, there is a desperate need to bring them into the work force. (Is it any wonder that when in some groupings of young people the unemployment rate is 40 percent, so many of them turn to crime?)

If, as some unions want, the age drifts down to fifty-five within the next ten years, the pressure on both society and individuals to make the retirement years rewarding and useful, perhaps opening out into "second careers," will be greatly intensified. And if in the same period, the scientists put us up to a life span of ninety or so, the pressure will really mount.

Perhaps the need for wisdom in confronting this problem is greater than in any other of all the sticky decisions we have to make. At sixty-five most of today's old have several years of fairly zestful living before genuine old age arrives. Lucky are they, I sometimes think, for whom the terrible decision of when to retire has been made by others – provided, of course, there is enough income to live on.

But the self-employed are up against this hardest of decisions. Doctors and lawyers, especially, face it, and some do very badly with it. Who has not know the respected elder who hung on too long and thereby lost the respect of all his coworkers? Because we have known him, the pressure is on us to "quit while the quitting is good." But knowing just when that time has come is not easy. The judge who hung on because he would be "just another old man" after retirement managed to stay on the bench until death took him, but for several years before his death every lawyer tried to avoid taking cases into his court.

People who hold jobs they like and excel at are nearly always surprised at how much of life seems to drop out at retirement. The job, they find, is much more than a forty-hour week topped off with a paycheck. A job you like and are good at is a means of personal growth, a way in which you can measure your personality and performance against those of other people. It identifies you as "belonging," as being in the mainstream of life, as a participant rather than a bystander. It gives structure to time, so that Monday feels different from Friday, midweek from weekend. ("Every day is Sunday," one of my sisters-in-law commented wryly after her husband's retirement. She missed the structured time when Sunday and vacations were special.) A job is also a place where one meets people and learns how to work with them, perhaps acquires friends among them. For all these reasons some gerontologists believe that retirement is the most traumatic experience many people ever have. For some people, however, it is release from a detested routine. And for those who have provided themselves something to retire to, the day of the Gold Watch marks the beginning of a satisfying new life phase.

Nowadays it is being said that we need more entry jobs for the young. So we do, but we also desperately need many more withdrawal jobs for the elderly, so that this particular withdrawal can be a staging-out of activity for those who still retain the vitality to make valuable contributions. America may be rich, but no society is rich enough both to support and educate its young until age 18 or later, and also to maintain a large and rapidly increasing number of its old in idleness. If we want to improve the conditions under which the elderly poor are condemned to live, therefore, we who have been fortunate have a responsibility to help find or make ways for our less fortunate contemporaries to have decent lives.

The decision to retire is usually made for us, but practically all the other hard decisions we face must be made for our-selves by ourselves.

"When shall I give up driving?" may seem a simple question, but in an era of poor (or nonexistent) mass trans-portation, turning in a driver's license means a loss of mobility that may be almost total. How is one to get to church or go to a volunteer job or visit an ailing friend? Take a bus? In my city, as in most today, the buses run to downtown but almost nowhere else that I ever want to go. Call a cab? Too expensive for most of us, and even though the rest of us may very well know that we can take a lot of cabs for what it costs to keep a car, most of us, having been brought up on the maxims of thrift and having battled our way through the Great Depression, find it really hard to summon a cab.

And while we are trying to make up our mind to give up the car, the traffic becomes fiercer by the month. Every time I wait for an opening to let me into the boulevard when I leave my garage, I watch those rushing lines of lethal steel with anxiety. Are my reflexes still quick enough? Is my judgment still good enough? Too often we waver in indecision until there is an accident, and the police or insurance company decides for us.

Because I have observed that many old people are inclined to argue our driving ability on the grounds of our cautiousness as contrasted with teenagers' reckless speed, it may be well to quote Dr. Birren again. After saying flatly that the over-seventy driver is more likely to have a highway accident than are drivers in the much discussed age bracket of 16 to 20 years, he goes on:

Many factors combine to make individual drivers over sixty-five more likely to have accidents: diminished visual acuity, less resistance to glare, hearing loss, and impairments of physical movements. Also the increased reaction time known to occur with age is involved, as drivers must respond quickly to unpredictable events.

These facts make the decision much tougher.

Another of the painful decisions for many old people is, "Should I give up my house and garden to move into an apartment?" This is one with which middle-aged sons and daughters are not apt to be very sympathetic. Having themselves moved about the country at the American rate, they often cannot understand why we cling to a house that has become hard to maintain and perhaps is in a deteriorating neighborhood. So they begin to urge: "Sell the house. It's too big for you and keeping up the garden has become too much for you. Move into an apartment near me where I can look in on you often."

All this we freely grant to be true. But to give up the house means a drastic change in our way of living. We've grown accustomed to space. How will we manage in the cubicles designated by apartment builders as "kitchen," "living room," and "bedroom?" And how can we fit our heavy old furniture into those cells? If we can't, can we bear to replace our accumulation of walnut and mahogany with what is now for sale in furniture stores?

And the garden! To be sure, it is only a city garden, snidely called a "pocket garden" by some larger-scale gardeners, but for years we have watched for its first crocus, waited to see what the new tulips will add to its design, separated the iris rhizomes, planted out the winter-housed geraniums, found a place for a few tomato plants and herbs, and taken meals out on a tray to enjoy whatever happened to be in bloom. How can we possibly give up that little piece of the earth where perhaps the children played, where a now-dead husband or wife helped with the planting and upkeep, and where we can be aware of all the many creatures that share it with us: the hummingbird pair, other birds feeding or nesting, the rascally squirrel who steals the rose hips and dogwood berries and has been known to ravish the tomato plants, the butterflies and the bees over the lythrum, the unseen worms under the grass, the repulsive sow-bellies, the occasional tortoise, or even a cottontail? To give up all this for a sterile apartment is hard. If all this sounds like the lament of a sentimental old woman, I plead guilty.

Still the house, and not the garden, is the main rub. If we go into an apartment how can we house the out-of-town family when they come? Or entertain old friends come for a visit? It's true, of course, that the family reunions are getting to be a strain on us, but can we bear to cut ourselves away from all chance of them? The younger grand-children, for instance, will miss most of the experience of visiting grandparents. And will the older grandchildren still want to come?

These are painful questions, but the decision is infinitely harder if, as often happens, a middle-aged son or daughter living in another town is urging us to take an apartment nearby. If we yield to their pressure, we will have to rely on them emotionally because it may be too late to build a place for ourselves in a new community. Can we weather this drop in status? Or will we fall swiftly into dependent old age? Frost was right when he said that "no memory of having starred atones for later disregard."

On the other hand, if we refuse the children and insist on taking an apartment in a community where we have friends, and a "place," the friends will be dropping off and we may ultimately be alone. Or we may have a long terminal illness and feel terrible guilt for making it so difficult for our children to care for us in a town halfway across the continent from them.

And after the apartment has been settled into, more withdrawals and detachments come on, with each of them trailing another set of hard decisions. The very interests most often urged upon the retired person – hobbies in the field of arts and crafts or volunteer work in the community bring on painful retirement decisions. That grand elder, Helen

Hayes, put it well in The Gift of Joy: "One doesn't want to hang about too long, pressing upon the world the gifts that have become a little damaged or tarnished by envious time." Exactly. But when?

Except for a few giants like Picasso and Casals, eventually the creative energy flags and our paintings or music (or writing, I must remind myself) lose their appeal to others. In the same way, the person who has acquired skills in community organization must be alert for signs that withdrawal from leadership is at hand. Younger people are needed on the boards and commissions. But the oldster's need to belong and to be respected for his contribution is no less than it always was; his need is perhaps even greater because of the detachments he is making in other areas. And when he bows out, how does he manage to continue making some kind of contribution to the common life, so that he can feel he is still pulling part of the common load? In other words, how avoid status drop, isolation, feelings of uselessness – in short, alienation?

COUNTERING THE TIME MILL

Time is, of course, a problem for everyone. But on no one does its mill grind so hard as on the old. In childhood it is infinitely slow, in youth considerably accelerated but still often dragging painfully. But for old people it seems fairly to whiz by, and each year seems to be shorter than the one before it.

Some scientists have suggested that this felt speed-up may be due to a slowing of the metabolic processes. Others think it the result of the old person's knowledge that for him time is almost gone, so he clings to it in a desperate attempt to halt it or at least slow it down somewhat. Whatever the cause, most old people in most centuries, and apparently in most cultures, seem to have felt that time was speeding up. Today, when the tempo of technological and social change has been accelerating wildly, the

148

coming together of racing external change and the slowing internal time make a very bad combination for the old. The effort to deal with it creatively is one of our very real struggles.

It is easy and perhaps instinctive simply to dig in one's heel and resist all change. Such resistance in the old is politely known as "rigidity" – and more colloquially as "cussedness." Throughout all history, right down to the twentieth century, this tendency of the old had a social function. By clinging to the old ways, they were the keepers of tradition, the transmitters of group values from one generation to the next.

But not now.

We may feel that having seen so much history in the making the best thing we have to offer is what we have learned during our long wrestling with circumstance. But today nobody wants either our memories or our numerous ideas on proprieties and procedures. Nobody. Not the young – they are, as always, engrossed in the present and the future. Not the middle-aged – they are too busy trying to bring the present into some kind of order. Not the intellectuals – most of them have concluded that in a time of tornadic change the future is all-important and the past of little value for guidance. Except for the handful of us who have made great contributions or achieved fame or notoriety of some sort, mighty few of us find any public for our memories or our multitudinous ideas for world improvement.

So if we are reasonably smart, we endeavor never, never to intone "Now, when I was young . . ." It's an effort, I assure all my juniors. And if we want any of them to enjoy being with us, we'd better at least try to be "flexible," instead of being that horrible "set-in-his-ways." But at the same time we are expected to be discriminative in our attitudes toward change. If we run full sail into every new fad or idea as a few seniors do, we are regarded as, at best, eccentric and, at worst, somewhat "cracked."

If time has always seemed to speed up

for old people, it has surely never in all history dealt with them so harshly as now, for never has any generation seen so much change in so many facets of life. Change is now so rapid and so all-pervasive that many old people simply cannot cope with it. Young people and even the middle-aged can have no real idea of what time has done and is doing to us and how severe is the effort to adjust to that doing.

Many, perhaps the majority, of us grew up among people who never got as far as a hundred miles from home. How could they prepare us for all the different sorts of humanity, the cultural differences, and the international hatreds that now tumble into our living rooms with the evening news. Or how could they get us ready for all the mechanical and social changes that have come into being in our lifetime?

Let me be a little personal about this. Most old people today can remember when automobiles were a rarity only the rich could afford. My own first beau drove a flashy horse-and-buggy, but I have lived to watch a horseless vehicle driven on the surface of the moon and a mechanical hand scraping up the red soil of Mars into a machine capable of chemical analysis. I well remember when the first telephone came into our rural neighborhood. It was a real miracle to be able to talk to a neighbor two miles away. But the jump from that hand-cranked box on the wall to communication between a Houston laboratory and an astronaut bouncing on the moon or even with our being able to talk with someone on the other side of the earth is really no greater than the jump from the devoutly held work-ethic of my childhood to the leisure-oriented life-style now coming into being. Then the Devil (a real personage) was known to be on the constant lookout for idle hands. Now we are being exhorted by equally confident mentors to get ourselves hobbies or intellectual interests or something to sustain us in the days ahead, when fifteen percent of the country's work force will be producing all the country's goods.

Or take another area. In our youth, males "doffed their hats" in the presence of females – only nobody ever, ever used the words "male" or "female" in "mixed company." Women could neither vote nor hold prestigious jobs or, in some states, even own property. Blacks were still generally held to be an inferior race, and nobody but Quakers and the most confirmed liberals seriously doubted that the only really good Indians were dead.

The jump from the attitudes toward sex in our childhood to those of today is really unbelievable. Our parents, be it always remembered, were reared in the Victorian era and many of us were born in its last years. Consequently, the whole subject of sex was swathed in taboos and never mentioned by women with any pretense to "refinement." Both my grandmothers, for instance, always referred delicately to my father's stallion or bull as "the animal." Even my mother's women friends had "limbs" instead of legs. My mother herself was a good horsewoman, but she never rode except sidesaddle. Riding astride would have forced her to choose between breeches and an immodestly pulled-up skirt.

Chastity in those days was a must. Nice girls allowed no courting liberties, and many brides went to the nuptial bed almost totally ignorant. An unmarried girl who became pregnant was "ruined," literally, unless the man married her, by choice or by force. Mention of venereal disease or abortion in the presence of "ladies" would have been a monstrous breach of etiquette.

Or take another whole area of life. From a world where thrift was one of the prime virtues and the admonition, "Waste not, want not," was constantly dinned into our youthful ears, we have moved to a world of credit cards and throwaways.

Or another area. Stealing, even very petty theft, was a sin and a dreadful disgrace. Now, in many circles, it is casually referred to as "ripping off."

These sharp jumps (and there are many others) daily confront the old, and always with the pressure to adjust, to "be flexible." The changes are so radical and so numerous that the economist Kenneth Boulding has asserted that "the world of today is as different from the world into which I was born as that world was from Julius Caesar's. I was born in the middle of human history. Almost as much has happened since I was born as happened before."[2]

In our lifetimes we have moved from a world that seemed permanent and with fixed values to a time of general flux and with expectations of still more radical changes just ahead. And because we are the first generation ever to be whipped about so furiously, we have no handed-down recipes for coping with today's gales of change. The wonder is that

2. Quoted by Alvin Toffler in Future Shock, p.15, from Boulding's speech at the Nobel Conference, Gustavus Adolphus College, 1966.

155

many of us do pretty well at it.

The reason others of us fail are summarized by Toffler in Future Shock:

Whatever the reasons, any acceleration of change that has the effect of crowding more situations into the experiential channel in a given interval is magnified in the perception of the old person. As the rate of change in society speeds up, more and more older people feel the difference keenly. They, too, become dropouts, withdrawing into a private environment, cutting off as many contacts as possible with the fast-moving outside world, and , finally, vegetating into death."[3]

COPING WITH ALONENESS

Old people are not "s'posed to be" sexually alive. If they are, and are so lucky as still to have their mates, the screen of marriage protects them from social attention. Who knows or cares

3. Alvin Toffler, Future Shock (New York, Bantam Books, 1970), p. 40.

what they do in their own bedrooms? (It is now well known that many old couples remain sexually active long after they used to be thought "beyond all that.") So the death of a spouse after a long and good marriage is not only the cruelest emotional loss one can suffer but initiates a subterranean deprivation rarely spoken of by the afflicted.

I once heard a widow in her eighties remark to a long-absent brother who was fondling her, "Thank you so much for this. I have such a hard time getting any loving." The sense of touch is a basic part of our emotional equipment. Quite apart from whatever need for sexual union still remains, the need for fondling, cuddling, hand-holding and cheek laid to cheek – for the comfort of head resting against breast, body enclosed in affectionate arms – this need does not disappear with the death of a mate. But it is a hard need for the old to gratify. Everybody loves to touch and fondle a rosy toddler – nobody is much driven to caress someone with a time-scarred face and thin, gnarled hands.

Once the first crush of grief has been absorbed, the survivor faces a new train of hard decisions: Shall I give up what remains of my sexual life? Shall I accept my deprivation and adjust to it by whatever means are open to me? Or shall I attempt to find another mate?

If the latter option is clearly not open, as it often isn't for widows past early middle age, the questions move on. Shall I give up my sexual life or shall I pursue it outside marriage despite society's decree that for old people such activities are either unspeakably absurd or downright nasty? The whole question has been so thoroughly explored by recent writers that there is no reason to go into much detail here. But perhaps a few words are needed.

The folk wisdom agrees with the Old Testament sage that there is "a time for all things," but it firmly adds that the time for making a new marriage or other sexual alliance is not in old age. And the belief continues that the individuals who defy that decree are proper objects of social mirth.

In this situation a widow's options are much fewer than those of a widower, because his chance for a satisfying re-marriage is so much greater than hers. Almost any elderly widower, if socially well placed or even just financially "comfortable," can remarry, often to a much younger woman. The December-May marriage of a Supreme Court justice or a United States Senator may inspire some jokes, but if he chooses to make that marriage, he can. And if it turns out to be rewarding to both parties, the jokes are easily tolerated.

But a widow of the same age, no matter how distinguished or "well preserved," has a much smaller chance to remarry. There are not only fewer men in her age bracket, but those few tend to marry younger women. Usually nothing but a good bank account or sheer luck will give her a chance – and even then she had better not be too choosy. In any case she will bring down on herself an avalanche of scornful ridicule if she is observed to be "making moves" or what used to be called "setting her cap."

To be widowed in our society is to be a social cripple. It is to be always and everywhere "an extra woman" or to associate exclusively with other women. It is being required to make many decisions one never had to make and undertake responsibilities one never had to carry (the car upkeep, for instance). It is to be not only sexually but emotionally deprived. It is having to come face to face with that great winnower of character – loneliness. For many widows it is not only to be alone but also to be desperately poor. Small wonder if some of them yearn for remarriage.

But as Beauvoir has described for all time, the very idea of an elderly woman seeking a new husband arouses universal scorn. Tongues wag and jokes fly if a widow is observed to be showing an interest in a man. As a bludgeon, "silly old woman" is every bit as crushing as "dirty old man."

Things are changing in this area as in every other aspect of life. In the retirement centers, today's widowers, particularly the well-to-do and the distinguished looking, are coddled and flattered outrageously, and eventually many of them succumb. According to HEW, about 35,000 over-65 marriages are now being made each year. Some of them stick, some don't, as in every other age group. Sometimes the idiosyncrasies of pension systems decree that the couple simply live together instead of marrying. But that too happens in all age groups.

Because of the prevailing social attitudes, the whole field of sexual activity in the old is only beginning to be studied. We are, however, becoming somewhat more knowledgeable about it. Dr. Leaf, for instance, was impressed by the number of post-centenarians in Abkhasia who still maintained an interest in sex. Several of them seemed to equate youth with sexual activity and said that up to ninety or so they had considered themselves "youth." One of them, aged 110, "admitted that he had considered himself a youth until "a dozen years ago." These were people who continued to do hard physical labor until over the century mark, who walked up and down mountain roads, and who never had a chance to become physically slack.

If the life span is about to be increased by even a few more years, the whole problem of emotional satisfaction through the sense of touch undoubtedly will intensify, no matter how sexual activity among the elderly comes to be regarded. Perhaps people now middle-aged should cultivate the fine art of hand holding in the hope that when their turn comes to be old they will have at least a chance to avoid the touch-starvation that now afflicts many old people. For too long "silly old woman" and "dirty old man" have been hurled at people whose basic error may have lain in being so starved for touching that they could not resist trying to satisfy their need.

CULTIVATING CHEERFULNESS

If he does not want to be confined to the company of his contemporaries, that is, segregated by age, the sensible elder makes a real effort to be cheerful. Always, and no matter how his arthritis is cutting up, his ego hurting, or his money running short. He cannot, this sensible elder, help knowing that cheerfulness is his passport to whatever general acceptance will be accorded him. Gloomy Gus and Anxious Annie are going to be given a wide berth by everyone who isn't either duty bound or paid good money to attend them.

So we try to give at least the impression of being happy. More than that, we try to be happy by reminding ourselves frequently of the many pluses in our lives. After all, we lecture ourselves, the world has quite enough misery without our adding to it. But along with the lecture we recognize that we'd better be cheerful.

If this sort of old person has a passionate desire left, it is that he may not become "a burden." Anyone who talks frequently to old people must be impressed with the unanimity with which they say, "I don't want to become a burden to my children." It is a refrain, a drumbeat running through almost every frank conversation with the elderly. We want, and want most fervently, to remain independent, not become a bother. And if, as the years go by, we sometimes become nuisances because of a faulty balance between independence and dependence, the error is usually on the side of trying to be more independent than we can be. After all, we get our falls when we are trying to do for ourselves instead of sitting in a rocker being waited upon.

As 82-year-old Florida Scott-Maxwell put it in the notebook that became The Measure of My Days: "I have a duty to all who care for me not to be a problem, not to be a burden. I must carry my age lightly for all our sakes, and thank God, I still can."[4]

It is a tribute to age that most of the best old people I have known take this "carrying my age lightly" quite seriously. One of their chief reasons for trying is to present a picture of it that can help to relieve some of the dread of age that haunts younger people.

Being cheerful in old age is no easy matter. It is a time for stout hearts and, what is worse, for stout hearts that are not going to be much noticed. Who still in the thick of life ever considers what it must take to face the fact that death is at best only a little way down the lane? Or the twin fact that if one lives to a really long old age, one is certain to be struck down again and again by grief? Stand beside a procession of coffins, one of them containing the body of a wife or husband? Become more and more alone and detached? And that almost every year can be counted on to bring on

4. Florida Scott-Maxwell, The Measure of My Days (New York: Alfred A. Knopf, 1960), p.31.

another handicapping, usually painful ailment?

But the final fear, the capping anxiety, that today's old must face because medical science has found out how to keep us alive long after our humanity is gone, is that one may become a mindless thing in some nursing-home bed. It happens, we cannot help seeing, all the time and to the saint as well as the reprobate. Perhaps science will some day be able to tell us how to avoid that fate, but today it is a specter in every elder's heart. As one of my friends put it, "I don't fear death, but I am desperately afraid of becoming one of the living dead."

In the face of all this, real courage is required just to get up in the morning and go about one's business. And this courage, let it not be forgotten, must be generated in the midst of a society that is only beginning to accept death as subject for conversation. What old person, trying to talk of this intimate concern, has not met a hearty, "You don't need to start worrying yet – you've still got many good years ahead of you." Cheering us up, they call it.

Yes, old age is a time for valor. We shan't be accepted if we're not cheerful. At the same time we can't in the very nature of things be cheerful without a fund of basic fortitude. And what is more, this fortitude is not going to win us any medals or even be much noticed. Whoever heard of an award for cheerfulness?

MAKING THE FINAL ARRANGEMENTS

During late old age, especially in what Dr. Larsen calls the "frail stage," thoughts of impending death cannot really be smothered, no matter how adept we have become at the process. At seventy-five, one doesn't have to be maudlin to think, "Not many years left. I'd better begin to put things in order." Thereupon, another whole series of decisions step forward.

"What arrangements should I be making?" Attitudes vary widely. Some old people say, "Let the family do what they like. I won't be around to see or care." Others want to plan their funeral service down to the last hymn. A New York Times obituary writer, who has interviewed many old people in order to prepare their obituaries in advance, has found that "many if not most older persons have little or no terror of death. . . . They accept it as inevitable. Many, indeed, have planned their funerals and picked out their burial sites."

While most of us do not go so far as to plan our funerals, all of us who are not too afraid of death begin to think about it in practical terms. If we are so lucky as to live in the vicinity of a son or a daughter and he or she will allow us to talk, the battle is eased. Perhaps the family already owns a burial plot. If not, shall we buy one and in which cemetery? Conventional funerals are increasingly expensive. Should we join one of the "sensible funeral" associations? Or perhaps settle for cremation? (On this last point discussion is especially important, for some members of the family may have strong feelings on the matter.) If cremation is acceptable to all, what disposition of the ashes?

Needless to say, the old person without near relatives who are at least somewhat younger will find "arranging things" especially difficult. In this connection I am reminded of a letter received from a man I knew when we were both graduate students at the University of Illinois. He never married, lived near an older sister, and had recently had a malignant lung tumor removed.

My sister and I have apparently each been depending upon the other for care when we get too old and weak to manage by ourselves. Obviously, I'll never be able to care for her; and she has so many ailments that she can't look after me. My doctor is already hinting that I should either get somebody to stay with me or else go into a home. . . . I'll go on this way as long as I can and then do the next best thing, whatever it should turn out to be.

Luckily for him, death came soon afterwards.

One's will may need to be overhauled because of changes in tax laws or the family situation. For this we will need a lawyer. If we don't already "have" one, whom shall we approach? Many a widow hangs up on the question of which attorney and dies with the out-dated will of her spouse.

Then there is the matter of special bequests. What can I do to make the disposition of my belongings easier for my family and prevent hurt feelings? One device used by some old people is to make lists and put them alongside the will. This, of course, will require such decisions as which granddaughter gets the tea service and which grandson would most appreciate Papa's chess set. Or if the children and grandchildren have apparently finished with frequent moves around the country, one can simply give them now the things one wants them to have eventually. If death is not to bring on family discord, all these matters involve a good deal of frank discussion.

In her last years my mother-in-law worked out a good system. First she gave back to the donors all but the most trivial gift articles she had received from them. Then on the bottom of family treasures she pasted a bit of adhesive tape and wrote upon each the initials of the one she wished to receive it. (Some of us had some surprises when we came to distribution day!)

Another method is simply to ask the family who wants this or that. If this or that is not really desired by anybody, we can call the Salvation Army or Good Will. Maybe even they won't want it! It may be like draining our heart's blood to see the article in the trash pickup, but the family will call us blessed on the day they must clear out the house or apartment. Garage sales will also get rid of an astounding amount of trivia.

Another whole set of decisions involves handling one's money. Towards the end of a really long life, most people begin to have trouble with their money – besides the usual trouble of there not being enough of it. On one level it may be fear of having a Social Security check stolen. On another it may be fear of having to make even minor financial decisions. Managing a checkbook, "keeping straight with the bank" may become a wearing and confusing business. Eventually, if the oldster has children in the vicinity, he may just decide that the effort is too great and say, "Here, you take care of it all." But to do this, he must trust the middle-aged son or daughter and, unfortunately, some are not trusted. Sometimes they are not trustworthy, sometimes the old person is overly suspicious. In any event, this can turn into one of the real tragedies of old age.

Handling of money often becomes a serious problem, even when there is not much of it to handle. Particularly for widows. They become afraid it "won't hold out and I'll be left with nothing but Social Security." In that case they may become miserly, afraid to spend even for genuine needs. Or they may get grandiose ideas and become a prey to any sharp salesman or promoter of a "good cause." For obvious reasons, widows are hit hardest by these decisions. (Too many of us have had no experience in handling money.) Some writers have humorously labeled the agonizing decisions over small financial problems "the widow syndrome." But elderly men, even those who have had good financial experience, may become penurious and afraid to spend or may overspend out of exaggerated notions of their financial worth. Money trouble may thus be one of the first symptoms of oncoming senility. A headache for all concerned.

Other hard decisions come if we decide to move into a retirement apartment or center. What do I want of it? All meals to be eaten in the common dining room? Or an apartment with a small kitchen where I can make at least my own breakfast and snacks? Must it have an infirmary and, if so, how well is it to be equipped and staffed? If the one near a son or daughter is inferior to one in another town, which shall I choose?

Finally, and nowadays one of the most important arrangements to be made, what do I do to prevent my being kept alive in some hospital bed long after my mind, which is to say my humanity, has gone? One answer, for old people sufficiently forthright to give it, is to send to family, doctor, lawyer, and minister or priest signed and witnessed copies of the statement worked out by the Euthanasia Educational Council:

If the time comes when I can no longer take part in decisions for my own future, let this statement stand as the testament of my wishes: If there is no reasonable expectation of my recovery from physical or mental disability, I request that I be allowed to die and not be kept alive by artificial means or heroic measures. Death is as much a reality as birth, growth, maturity, and old age – it is the one certainty. I do not fear death as I fear the indignity of deterioration, dependence and hopeless pain. I ask that medication be mercifully administered to me for terminal suffering even if it hastens the moment of death.

This request is made after careful consideration. Although this document is not legally binding, you who care for me will, I hope, feel morally bound to follow its mandate. I recognize that it places a heavy burden of responsibility upon you, and it is with the intention of sharing that responsibility and of mitigating any feeling of guilt that this statement is made.

There are other hard decisions, of course. Battalions of them. But these I have listed are surely enough to indicate that old age is no "placid sea." Middle-aged people had better be getting themselves together in preparation for weather just as stormy as any they have ever experienced. Ilya Ehrenburg, the Russian writer, once remarked on the basic difficulty facing old people:

For the past fifteen years or so, I have been learning how to be an old man. This is not nearly as easy as I thought when I was young. I used to think that desires die down along with the possibilities of satisfying them; but then I began to understand that the body ages before the spirit and that one has to learn to live like an old man. One learns even in dying; to die in such a way that death is a fitting end to one's life is not an easy art.

Part II

6

But There Are Some Pluses

Thus far we have been talking about the debits, the minuses of old age, and heaven knows their roster is formidable. As we went through the gloomy list it may have seemed that the state of being old is completely bleak. For many lonely, poverty-crushed, disease-ridden old people it is indeed very nearly that.

But as I move further along into old age and talk with other old people, I am discovering that for many if not most of us there do come, along with the painful limitations and withdrawals, some real compensations. Having said the words, I feel like fingering my rabbit's foot, for something dreadful may hit me any year, any month – and then I may be hard put to find any pluses. But meantime I am discovering and enjoying them.

It cannot be said too strongly that the minuses are real and that our society is not doing what it could and should to cushion the sufferings of many older Americans. But because of the prevailing horror of old age and because most of the writers on the subject are compassionate young or middle-aged people themselves affected by that horror, very little has been said about even the possibility of there being anything on the credit side of old age. In today's intellectual atmosphere, something almost like a taboo appears to surround discussion of the pluses. For instance, Gail Sheehy's recent book, Passages: Predictable Crises of Adult Life, does not discuss old age as one of the crises, indicating no doubt that we are not considered adult. Few believe or even seem to want to believe that anything good can be said about the state of being old. Hence, when one goes to write of the pluses, the words tend to sound either "preachy" or badly dated. In this day and age moralizing doesn't go down well – but some of the pluses are based on propositions the philosophers have always been moralizing about. Easier, oh much easier, for a writer to stick to the minuses. But let me try the pluses.

Old age is only a stage of life – like infancy, childhood, youth, or middle age. Like all the others, it is a time of change in both body and person, and like any time of change, it brings the possibility of growth. It can also be, and too often is, a time of withering away, or to use the scientists' word, retrogression. But it doesn't have to be. Everybody has seen people who kept on growing right through old age. It can be a time when the personality comes into its final bloom. Like all the preceding stages, it has some pluses – always providing we do not encounter an overwhelming disability and that we do have the essentials outlined earlier. (Sufficient income to provide adequate diet, housing, and medical care – and then the wit and the will to make the income really yield those essentials; an active mind and some genuine interests; self-esteem; a feeling of being needed and useful; and a basically life-loving attitude.)

Those qualities, I realized as I wrote them down, are either identical to or very close to those Abraham Maslow outlined as "basic needs," the satisfaction of which permits us to move on to what he calls gratification of "Meta-needs" in which the individual is devoted to some task or vocation and lives in a feeling of great luck. (His words for the basic needs were belongingness, affection, respect, and self-esteem.)

To claim the pluses is not to go the whole way with Browning contemplating old age from the safety of his middle years: "The best is yet to be, for which the first was made," Such optimism is realistically impossible for any but the most favored, most highly developed of us. But there are, nevertheless, some real credits that help to balance off the debits.

These compensations, however, do not come to us on any silver platters.

Indeed, we had better keep it firmly in mind that nothing much is likely to be handed to us except money enough to keep us alive. We must look for the rewards and, having found them, we must carefully build them into the framework of our everyday attitudes and habits. The struggle to perceive and enjoy them is harder for some types of personalities than for others. The "activist," for instance, may find it a harder undertaking than his more reflective friend.

One of the first rules of the search for pluses is not to go digging among the wise sayings of the past. Talk about the "crown of glory" and "authority of age" may have applied to some of the elders of ancient Israel or Rome, but it hasn't the first tiny thing to do with the American old of the 1970s. Beyond our Social Security payments we must discover or create for ourselves whatever velvet there is to be had in our old age.

Another good rule for the search is that finding a plus is not enough. It must be thought about, walked around, turned over in the mind, absorbed into the person, enjoyed. If this sounds like just another musty admonition to count one's blessings, so be it. The Senior who has thought about his blessings is likely to be much better company than the one who sits and mourns his troubles – and he, therefore, is much less likely to be lonely.

Thinking about and absorption of the pluses can be a highly creative process. Remember, we are excluded from success in the values most cherished by American society: youth, productivity, progress, competitiveness. Because we are thus excluded, we elders who wish to be happy must either have or create values appropriate to our stage of life. And then we must judge ourselves by how well we live by them instead of by the general standards. For this reason some students of old age have gone so far as to call the old "a deviant group." The phrase sounds bad, but it is expressive. Judged on the scale of the general

American social values, we are worthless. Judged on another scale we can be extremely useful. Because we're off the labor market, we can never again "compete" or "achieve" in the usual ways. If we accept these generally accepted values, we are forced to think of ourselves as worthless.

But there are other values. It is my belief that nobody has looked with sufficient realism at those values that many of us are creating for ourselves. Or at the new pleasures and freedoms that come to us with the years. It is, I think, time and past time that we stop bemoaning our fate and begin to assert the pluses.

7

The Pleasures of Grandparenthood

Becoming a grandparent for the first time is a big emotional experience, usually first met in middle age. But if we had more than one child and they married at different times, the appearance of new grandchildren and, eventually, great-grandchildren is an experience covering many years. Welcoming in a new generation is, take it from me, an almost dizzing experience. As I walked out of the hospital that morning of the first grandchild, I knew at last what the word "giddy" means. My feet seemed not quite to touch the ground!

We don't need to become self-conscious or hide our feelings just because the not-yet-old regard them as comic. Grandmother jokes are almost as ubiquitous as Scotchman or psychiatrist jokes. Grandfathers do not figure so largely in the folk humor, but they are equally and sometimes more absurd. About all that can be said for us is that most of us know that we are absurd and couldn't care less.

In the face of all this, why has grandparental love been so little written about? In all the 2,140 close-packed columns of my copy of Bartlett's there are only seven quotations about grandparents, male or female. And none of those pertain to the experience itself. In view of all the millions of pages that have celebrated young love and married love and illicit love and parental love, it really seems strange that so little has been said about grandparental love and that in our culture it is something to be joked about. Perhaps it is time for one of us to analyze it a bit.

Some of its quality is undoubtedly conveyed by the old cliché, "all the pleasure and none of the responsibility." Although Margaret Mead has taken us severely to task for that irresponsibility, it is for most of us at least part fact. Being a parent involves a staggering amount of work. The days are crammed, and in the early months no night yields unbroken sleep. If there are several children, this means that for a period of years somebody must maintain perpetual vigilance against the hazards of infection, accident, and mischief-making. The typical grandparent is a little smug in his reflection that he has served his turn at all the messy chores, back-breaking lifting, unremitting watchfulness, broken sleep, noise and confusion. All such matters are for parents, he thinks.

Besides all the work and responsibility, most modern parents have to carry quite a load of guilt feelings. The child, being human, misbehaves, and the parent, being human, flares into anger. A good part of the time the child feels better for the explosion, but the parent practically always feels guilty for his failure not only in patience but in his image of what a good parent ought to be.

Not the grandparent. He watches the outrageous conduct and is amused to remember when one of the young rebel's parents behaved exactly so – and lived to become a good citizen. He may even take a naughty satisfaction from this turn of life's wheel. Well do I recall how annoyed my sister and I used to be with our mother in her response to our worry over certain flaws appearing in our children's characters. "It's a judgment of the Lord on you," she would say with a mock-pious twinkle. When my daugheer's children showed signs of being fractious, I did not use the word judgment, but I confess to feeling very twinkly! Grandparents have had a long time in which to observe, as did an old aunt of mine, that "a lot just comes out in the wash." Meaning: many troublesome traits are only signs of growing up and will disappear in the natural course of events.

The grandparent is basically a spectator. He can enjoy the experience of watching life repeat itself in a new time and place. In an emergency or to give the parents a needed respite, he may volunteer to pinch-hit briefly. But when a tired child begins to be obstreperous, his likely reaction is to say, "It's time now to go home to Mommy." He loves the wonderful drama of budding (and erring!) humanity, but all that incessant work and responsibility are strictly for parents, thank you.

On the other hand, years of watching people move from childhood to adolescence to maturity and finally to old age, have taught the grandparent that some things are not likely to come out in the wash. At such times, if he is near enough and wise enough, he can be a real resource for the generations under him. In any case he can let go and love the child or youth as he or she is. That kind of disinterested love is almost impossible for parents, who are apt to be unnerved by responsibility, but very possible for onlooking grandparents. It may be just what the child or youth needs.

It is my experience, however, that the bromide about pleasure and non-responsibility only touches the surface of the experience. I was prepared to enjoy my spectator status, for everybody talks about that. But nobody told me how my eyes would swim when I first saw the baby at her mother's breast and noticed that the expression on my child's face had become maternal. Nobody told me how excited I would be at each new small accomplishment or what swelling delight I would feel when a toothless grin announced that I was recognized. Nor was I prepared for the fun it would be to converse with budding minds that seem-ed to enjoy my stories of "how it was." I knew from my own childhood that listening to tales of a parent's childhood can be a means of widening a small child's sense of reality. That the godlike, Benign-Giant figure he knows as Daddy or Mommy was once small and defense-less as he feels himself to be, once had adventures like his own, once made mistakes and got into trouble just as he does – all this is like a reassuring fairy tale. I knew it to be a service the child needs, but nobody had given me the faintest idea of what fun it would be to supply the service.

Neither had anybody prepared me for the way I would treasure and carefully write down the droll remarks made in great seriousness that reveal how differently a child's mind functions from that of an adult. Nor with what tender concern I would later watch them thread their way among the pitfalls of adolescence. All this was new to me, because when I was being a parent, I was too busy and too involved to indulge myself in them.

Such emotions are pure joy, adulterated by nothing. They are a wonderful new dividend clipped from the long investment of work and love that went into one of the children's parents. Here are new human beings starting on their long journey. A new generation is on its way and I am so incredibly lucky as to be near enough to observe it. Time, for me, is merging into eternity. But I am part of it, and why should I mind?

This onlooker-identification with the object, unmarred by any need to possess it or to fret over it is, I think, akin to the aesthetic experience. Beyond even that, it is an overpowering fresh sense of the mystery and the miracle of life as it sweeps from generation to generation, returning again and again upon itself, but is never quite the same.

Ah, sweet foolishness of life, grandparents know much more about you than they did when they were younger!

8

A Gift of Some New Freedoms

FROM THE ALARM CLOCK
Next to the pleasure of watching a new generation appear in one's life, the most obvious compensation is the new freedoms that come alongside the disadvantages of retirement. Liberation from the alarm clock may not be a very noble freedom, but for many people it is a real one.

Lately we have begun to hear much about employee discontent. Indeed, this discontent appears to be one of the facts of contemporary life. Some of the recent studies of dissatisfaction among assembly line workers testify strongly as to how bitterly the pressures of quotas, repetitive small tasks, and driving supervisors are resented. For instance, Studs Terkel once taped an interview with a laborer in a Chicago steel plant. Among other things this assembly line worker said:[1]

I hope to God I never get broken in, because I always want my arms to be tired at 7:30 and 3 o'clock. 'Cause that's when I know that there's a beginning and there's an end. That I'm not brainwashed. In between, I don't even try to think. . . . Unless a guy's a nut, he never thinks about work or talks about it. . . . It's hard to take pride in a bridge you're never gonna cross. . . . The first things happen at work is that when the arms start moving the brain stops.

Why wouldn't such a worker, trapped in a dull and physically exhausting job, look forward to an end to such servitude?

But assembly line workers are not the only ones in that box. Executives speak emotionally of the "rat race." Office workers refer to the fifth day of the work

1. New Times, November 2, 1973, pp. 50-51.

week as "good Friday" and Monday as "blue." A recent survey came up with the startling statement that only 43 percent of all white collar workers really enjoy their work. And that most of even those who generally like their jobs have spells of feeling bound and driven by them. Thus for almost everyone the alarm clock is a symbol of all the years of stumbling foggily through the moring chores, half or wholly dreading the day ahead.

The less any worker likes his job, the more he is apt to dream of the day when he can shed it. He may not have the mistiest notion of what he will do with his time except "plenty of rocking and fishing," but how he longs to be free! A research worker at Pennsylvania State College once interviewed many railroad workers about their plans for retirement and was surprised to find that they had no plans for doing anything beyond taking a "good rest" and then a trip on their railroad passes.

In recent years some large

corporations have set up programs to "prepare" their older workers for retirement. One company interviewed its sixty- to sixty-five-year-old workers and found many of them saying in so many words that they were simply going to rock and fish. This was not surprising, but the second interview of these same employees made five years after retirement found that those who had planned just to "rock and fish" seemed to be happier and better adjusted than their more ambitious and carefully planning fellows. Perhaps they were just more easygoing and therefore happier by temperament. Or perhaps they had a better appreciation of silenced alarm clocks!

After all the years of morose obedience to the screaming tyrant on the bedside table, how wonderful to wake up in our own good time as animals do – and as preindustrial man could do if he liked. On snowy mornings what luxury to stretch catlike in a warm bed while listening to the neighbors battle reluctant cars. And to know that one no longer has to buck traffic and then face either an unreasonable supervisor or a goldbricking underling! The mood of the whole day changes after such a beginning.

For driving, ambitious people this change in awakening habits may be very hard to adjust to. In fact, I've known some who kept right on waking at the usual time without the alarm, and then feeling either empty or guilty because they were being "lazy." (Whenever you look at an old person, you are probably seeing someone in whom the good old "work ethic" was early instilled.) Housewives, whose husbands and children had to have early breakfasts, tend to welcome wholeheartedly the new emancipation from the thing that hustled them out of bed five mornings a week. I know, for I was one of the lucky souls who, after the children were gone, was permitted to find my own rising hour while a celebrate-the-dawn type husband happily got himself organized for his day. Take it from me, it's a wonderful relief to have an alarm screeching only on the mornings when something special is scheduled.

For some of us, I might add, the break in rising habits may lead into what almost seem to be personality changes. An individual who was basically intellectual but through the accident of circumstances was shunted into a vocation demanding mostly muscular activity may surprise himself and his friends by becoming a "heavy reader" or by enrolling in a course in history or philosophy. On the other hand, if he was basically someone needing to use his muscles, but perhaps because of his family's social position spent his life behind a desk, he may make himself a "second career" in sailing or sculpture or serious gardening or something else that calls for physical exertion. For such people the first chance to be really themselves comes after the time when a clock starts and ends the day.

FROM THE STRESSES
OF COMPETITION

Some Americans seem to be "born competitors." They appear to need to outdo others: win the games and the prizes, make more money, acquire more status, "go up" faster and faster. Many of them seem to enjoy the competition for itself, especially if they are successful in it and are therefore able to push up their self-esteem to the desired level. (If unsuccessful, they may end up as the pathetic Willy Loman.) Playing the game hard and winning it seem to be the driving motors of their lives. For all such born competitors retirement may be a disaster, not only for the drop in status and income, but for the goalless hours likely to come with it. (This may be the reason women of my generation seem to move into old age easier than men do. Many of us never really had work-related goals.)

But for some people getting free from the necessity to compete may be a real boon. Their values or principles may have conflicted with those of the organization or the individual employer. Hence, they have resented or even felt torn by having to "toe the line" laid down for them. Freedom to abide by their own standards may be a real blessing. For such retirees being free just to be themselves with no more necessity to "impress" anybody is a secret delight. They never really cared much about keeping up with the Joneses anyway, and now they don't have to try. It was always a strain to push for the next promotion, and now they can relax. If they didn't respect the boss very much, he can now go jump in the nearest lake. Or maybe some of their colleagues, bucking hard for promotion, were treacherous. They too are for the lake, and good riddance.

Even those of us who were early and thoroughly indoctrinated in the divine attributes of work and the supreme value of "getting ahead" sometimes find to our surprise that the new drop in status is at least partly balanced by the new comforts. Among which I would certainly have to list the knowledge that whatever one was going to produce or accomplish is probably done or not done. We've either got it made or we haven't, and from here on out we're not expected to compete. In fact, if we produce or accomplish anything worthwhile, it will be cause for wonder and admiration in the populace around us.

There are other comforts. I once caught my recently retired husband looking at a picture of himself behind his big desk. Full of all the stories about the sufferings of new retirees, I asked sympathetically if he missed the excitement and status. "No," he replied in a tone much like the one he probably used when his mother caught him in the cookie jar, "I was just being glad that I don't have to go down there and face all the problems." He could confess to me, but I doubt if to anybody else.

Even if she is given to lamenting her uselessness now that the children have gone, the elderly housewife can also relax and may, if she is honest with herself, find it rather nice to be done with the responsibilities they laid upon her. Few grandmothers are so noble that they can listen to a daughter or daughter-in-law worrying with obstreperous young without smirking a bit over being through with all that. And if her husband was employed in a capacity that often uprooted the family, she may openly rejoiced at finally being able to settle down in a place of the family's own choosing – and be free from fretting with drapes that never seem to fit the new windows. Or if his job meant her having to "entertain" a good deal and be socially involved with the wives of his associates, she may discover that being "out from under all that" is a freedom not to be sneezed at.

Enjoying one's emancipation from today's workaday world may not be anything to be proud of, but it can be enjoyed – and I for one don't mind doing so.

FROM THE NECESSITY TO ACQUIRE

Almost everyone in my generation of Americans was brought up to believe in the necessity to acquire. One should "get ahead" and proof of that getting ahead was visible in the things one acquired. Nowadays some young Americans seem to have made nonacquisitiveness into a social virtue. In this way it has become an important ingredient in "the generation gap." But in our day only the really offbeat – such as bums, artists, and the professional religious – were free from the need to acquire. Men struggled and sometimes killed themselves in the effort to acquire bank accounts, pretentious houses, stocks and bonds, and luxury cars. Their wives struggled to acquire good carpets and sterling silver, impressive furniture, and the look of elegance in their clothing. Many a woman, whose husband could not give it all to her ready-made, learned to sew well, to refinish furniture, and to make her own slipcovers – or went out to earn money to purchase these things for herself. For both men and women the acquisition of each new item in the prescribed list was a personal triumph.

Here again the rebellion of some of to-day's young people has tended to soften the old compulsion. But even in my time there was a real difference among us in the degree of acquisitiveness. Some of us went along only to the point of achieving a modest competence and presenting a "decent" appearance. For all such among us, retirement gives an excuse to do as we like. The modest competence has been secured, Social Security is here for a floor, savings or pension will open a window or two, why kill ourselves in the probably vain effort to achieve more possessions and more notice? And besides, acquisitiveness may have begun to conflict with another of our ground-in values: thrift. The house is already cram-full, we tell ourselves complacently to cover the fact that we simply hate throwing anything away in order to make room for something else.

205

For such seniors finally getting free from the need to acquire can be a real relief. Unless we belong to the special breeds known as "collectors" and "compulsive shoppers," we are freed, or nearly so, from the need or the desire to add to our possessions. One of my own old age pluses is the fact that even including the Christmas buying spree, I now average less than three hours a month shopping for anything but groceries – and they cost me no more than five hours a month. For some people shopping is a form of entertainment; for me it was always a boring necessity to be postponed as long as possible. Now, at last, I can get happily by with very little of it and still feel "decent," that is, just sufficiently conforming to escape ridicule.

For nonacquirers it is a relief not to have to be constantly moving up in housing or jobs or cars. Instead of worrying about rebuilding the patio because our friends have done theirs over or redoing the kitchen because it has become a little tired looking, one can just shuck off the whole business, and who's to note or care? Oldsters are not expected to bother their heads about such matters anyway. But to feel this freedom as a "plus," we have to think about it a bit instead of alibiing about how our feet hurt nowadays when we shop.

Why not just admit it: possessions do not give us the thrill they once did. The silver stays in its tarnish-proof chest while we set our tables with stainless steel. The car has become just a means of transportation. And often, when someone makes us a gift of a handsome but sizable object, behind our smiles and grateful words we are groaning, "Something else to take care of. And where on earth shall I put it?" (When I made this confession to an elderly friend, he said, "My wife and I add another question: Whom can we give it to?")

FROM SOME OF THE PRESSURES TO CONFORM

If he wishes, the old person is excused

from a good many social demands. Grandma is not expected to keep up with every vagary of fashion. When spike heels are in style, nobody expects her to wear them; and in fact if she does totter forth on them, people will find the sight highly amusing. And when heavy square toes and high platforms are in, nobody expects her to risk her neck in them. Similarly, if Grandpa has never been a real, true-blue sports enthusiast, he is now freed from having to keep up with the sports records in order to talk with the fellows at work. If they both enjoy duplicate bridge, as one of my sisters and her husband do, they can join clubs and play exactly as much or as little as they like and not a single eyebrow will lift.

Granted reasonably good health and income, we over-65's are freer than ever before to set a life-pattern of our own choosing. If we elect to sit home and watch television, nobody is going to criticize us, though some will be sorry for the choice. But if we elect to go back for a high school diploma or college degree, at least some people will applaud us enthusiastically.

When we attempt to make use of this new freedom, however, it's a big help if we have had at least a little experience of nonconformity. We need to have tried at least a few times to discover our own way. Grandma Moses, be it remembered, had had some previous experience with pen and brush. And by all accounts she had always been a spunky soul who thought her own thoughts and dreamed her own dreams.

Even the cases when sudden blossoming seems to occur are probably not so sudden as they appear. For instance, in March, 1972, a retired seventy-one-year-old railway ticket agent confounded all his friends by enrolling as a freshman in Southern Illinois University. To a newspaper reporter he explained that about two years earlier he had retired and lost his wife. He "didn't want to sit down, dry, and blow away." Having always wanted to go to college, he "figured this was my chance." Such an attitude in a newly widowed retiree in his seventies is refreshing. But his next remark was downright staggering:

So far I haven't run into anything I wasn't fairly familiar with, but I told my counselor that as soon as I stop enjoying it I quit. At my age you're nuts if you keep on doing something you don't enjoy.

It sounds as if he had made a sharp break with his past. But does anyone think that somebody who has been out of school since he was fifteen, as this man had been, can pass his university entrance exams and then go on to make straight A's in his first college year if he had not been keeping his mind alive during all the intervening years? This may be as good a place as any to comment that a good sprinkling of retired people are now going to school to finish an interrupted education. I have, for instance, a sister-in-law who went back to college to graduate just fifty years from the time she dropped out to get married. Her husband (he who now rides the buses and planes) went along with her and they lived in the married students' quarters. Could they have taken this unconventional step if they had spent their half century in "going along?" I don't think so.

Several of my acquaintances have gone back to college after the death of a husband or wife. One in particular is worth noting. Ever since she left college to marry in her freshman year she had been feeling disadvantaged because her husband and all his friends were college graduates. (I have often thought that one of the chief values of a college degree is that with it one can't feel inferior over not having it!) She may never "use" the degree to better herself financially, but the process of getting it was invaluable for her self-esteem during the difficult period of losing husband and children at about the same time.

Another acquaintance demonstrated

what an older woman can do. I first knew Dorothy Hill Larsen, a Gerontology Fellow, when we were students and teaching assistants together in the graduate school of the University of Illinois back in the Twenties. She married and brought up her family, then took another master's in a completely different field, and finally, at age 62, completed her doctorate. Now at 79 she is still happily pursuing her "second career," conducting workshops and seminars in her special interest – the relationship of the middle-class older person and his church.

Even though I had several of these late matriculants in my own circle of friends and family, I have been surprised recently to learn how many of them there may be. During the last few years David Raskin of Evanston, Illinois, has been clipping stories about them from the New York Times and the Chicago Sun-Times. Although the file is undoubtedly far from inclusive, it contains twenty-two stories about oldsters whose setting out after a degree or securing of it came to the attention of these two papers.

Here are some samples of the headlines.

Ft. Myers, Florida: "Florida businessman, 57, starts work on a law degree."

Rampana, New Jersey: "Great grandmother, 67, becomes college freshman."

Chicago: "After 56 years he completes college work."

Arcato, California: "Couple graduates after 47-year wait."

Brooklyn, N.Y. "Life begins at 75." (This is the story of a freshman enrollee at Kingsborough Community College.)

Salt Lake City: "New co-ed, 82.

Fresno, California: "Woman, 81, seeking a college degree."

Edgefield, California: "Man, 79, gets diploma."

Elyria, Ohio: "Ohio freshman, 85, bridges school gap."

New York City: "Woman realizes dream and enters City U. at 83."

Detroit: "Ph.D. is the target of septuagenarian."

Long Island: "At 63 she still wants to be a doctor." (This is the story of a woman who knows she cannot now become an M.D. because of her age, but hopes to win a Ph.D. in the related field of biology. Since she already has a master's, she will probably reach her goal.)

In 1972 the University of California at Los Angeles had eleven over-70 students in a random sampling of 5,000 students. True, the number of such freewheeling elders is very small in comparison to either total university enrollment or our own numbers. But for every oldster who gets into print in this fashion, there must be many who don't. Which leads me to believe that quite a few of us must be defying the folk wisdom about the inability of old brains to learn. It would be a social disgrace if the current rise in college costs puts the experience out of reach for the increasing numbers of us who might pluck up the courage to try.

In the last few years, however, I have been delighted to note that a good many states have opened their universities tuition-free to the elderly. But we shouldn't think that even without tuition it will be easy, even if we can scrape up the money for books and other incidentals. With us there is always the fear of money running out during a long terminal illness and the nagging fear that maybe the folk wisdom about old brains may be right after all.

To return again to the seniors who have always tended to conform, to "go along," they may find it hard even to know what they would like to do. Too many of them, and especially the women among them, have never thought in terms of what they need or would like for themselves. So their tendency is to drift along in the same old pattern. Meantime, the special old-age pressures keep descending upon them, such as the two already discussed – cheerfulness and flexibility. The only seniors who don't feel these two pressures are those who live unto themselves and enjoy doing it.

Similar new demands keep right on coming along. "Be careful," we are admonished. "You don't want to break a hip, do you?" Or, "Watch your diet, dear." Or, "Do you think you should still be going up the stepladder?" And so on. Bless them, everybody who cares about us seems intent on helping to fit us into the usual pattern of old age. And even if they nobly abstain from the cautioning, as my family did, one may fall and have to spend months of painful convalescence while the broken pelvis or shoulder heals. Believe me, that teaches one to ease off!

Some of the demands can be somewhat relaxed by a humorous attitude toward ourselves and our doings. This business of our attitude toward ourselves is crucial. If we can find those precious selves, quirks and all, both worthy of respect and amusing, we are halfway home.

In today's world this attitude is not easy. Because our great need for the respect of others as a support for our own shaky self-respect is intensified by the mounting birthdays, we tend to shut our eyes to those of our personal traits that are less than admirable. Laugh at them as just another evidence of our being human? Horrors! So, on the theory that what we don't see or don't admit seeing amiss in our precious selves nobody else will notice, we tend to be very protective about them and very touchy about any spoken or unspoken criticism of them. And then, the first thing we know we have acquired a reputation for selfrighteousness. And rigidity. And being "difficult." And the next thing we know we are lonely and isolated, not having much fun in life.

The ability to laugh at one's self, while stoutly respecting that same self, will generate quite a bit of tolerant acceptance. It really will. If our clay feet are not too repulsive and do not come into view too often, friends and family may say indulgently, "It's one of her little-old-lady days," or, "He really got out of bed on the wrong foot this morning!" But to win that tolerance, the old person must have first understood in the deepest part of himself that there is nothing sacred about this or that pet idea – not even if it was acquired sixty years ago and has seemed to be reinforced during all the intervening ups and downs of life. Such understanding is, of course, a very large order that should have been started on much earlier.

To repeat: in ages, as in all other periods, much depends on our attitude toward ourselves. If we can't endure having our ideas challenged, if we want life to stay just as it was when we were developing tactics for coping with it, we are surely going to be known as "difficult." Difficult for ourselves and for everybody around us. And the number of those around us will be a lot smaller than it might otherwise have been. Worst of all, we are particularly guaranteed to become more difficult as time goes on.

If we're 100 percent sure that the

political, social, and religious ideas into which we were initiated are written into the immutable laws of the universe, we were born into the wrong century! The past wasn't all gold, and the troublesome present is not all base metal. If young people are "shacking up" as they didn't in our youth, a large percentage of them seem to be also more idealistic and more committed to humanity than we were. If the woman's movement is putting strains on the traditional family, we are not called upon to feel that the end of the world is at hand or that men and women will stop needing each other or that children either will stop appearing or will be reared on some kind of conveyor belt. If a Watergate hits, the country is not necessarily "rotten to the core," as I have heard numerous elders proclaim. It may just be getting a good push toward reforming some of its political ways.

Unthinkable as the idea is, we might occasionally think that we, and more especially our ideas, could be wrong. Our years are supposed to have given us perspective and even a modicum of wisdom. Surely, after a lifetime of watching the human creature perform or fail to perform, we should know that "there are more things in heaven and earth than are dreamt of" in our philosophy. It just might pay us to venture out in search of some of those things. Some of us would be amazed to find how liberating the search would be – and many of our juniors would applaud us for it.

If we panic at the thought of venturing out of our nice little lagoons where everybody thinks alike and behaves alike, we shall miss one of the important pluses of old age, the chance for growth. The beauty of it is that unless our adventurousness becomes really outrageous, it will actually be admired or at least smilingly tolerated. At our age we really are "nuts if we keep on doing what we don't enjoy" without putting up a fight to find something we do enjoy.

FROM MANY ILLUSIONS CHERISHED IN OUR YOUTH

When I was growing up in southern Kansas, I was absolutely sure that I was destined to break out of the Flint Hills and become famous for something – I didn't know what, but was certain that it was something wonderful. I dreamed that even though female, I would wander around the world seeing and tasting life to the full. I was sure that never again would my country be so foolish as to let itself be entrapped into a big war like the one in which my two grandfathers had fought. I believed that human nature is good, or would be if it could only learn how to manage its affairs just a little better. That within my lifetime, humanity would be wise enough to solve its chief problems and that I would have a small part of the solution. That science was pure benefactor. That we were on an endless escalator called "progress" which would inevitably carry us upward and forward to a good life.

So what happened?

221

I have lived the life of a middle-class housewife and community worker. I have been through two World Wars, a Cold War, Korea, and Vietnam. Electronic inventions, jet engines, nuclear energy, antibiotics and many other innovations have come along to change the whole texture of my life. And every evening at the flick of a button, problems of a complexity and magnitude the smartest of Ivy League professors couldn't or at least didn't imagine only thirty years ago come tumbling in upon me.

Of course not all young people in my generation were so unrealistic in their views of life and the future. But World War I had its effect on all of us, even if we never wore a uniform. Thanks to it, in the Twenties, we danced the Charleston, read Fitzgerald and Hemingway, worried about the League of Nations, and "settled down" still full of all sorts of worries about things that never happened and non-worries about psychotic German corporals. Some of our youthful dreams and illusions and fears were hard to part with. Now that I am old it is fun to remember them, but much better to be free from them.

By the time we are seventy, we know that most of our dreams are not going to be realized. The pain of failure has long since been absorbed, and, let's face it, the memory of the dreams have become a delicious part of a past that contained some thoroughly undelicious items. We can now feel toward those unrealized dreams much as we feel toward our first love, which no matter how un-substantial is now recollected with tender affection for the immature self of that day. Then life was a tray of candies. Now we know that right alongside the sweets are potions bitter as gall. Life has pounded into us the knowledge that there are no times and no places where one can live without distress. Then when we ran into trouble we thought it to be temporary, just a short run of bad luck. Now we know that all through life good and bad luck are interwoven. Now we know that William Blake was speaking truth in a triplet, short on poetry but very long on verity:

Man was made for Joy and Woe:
And when this we rightly know
Through the world we safely go."

By our time of life we have also learned, or should have that there are no panaceas, no social or physical cure-alls as we thought in our youth. We have watched the extension of the vote to women, black people, and eighteen-year-olds, all without any apparent increase in political rectitude. We have seen the end of city bosses herding workingmen to the polls at a slug of whisky and a dollar a head, although lately we have been seeing corporations and labor unions pay out huge sums in order to influence elections.

But we have also seen that in this immense, diverse country of ours, careful organization and the efforts of many citizens working together can, over a period of time, at least mitigate social evils. We have observed that patience and organization can win enough converts at least to reduce almost any social injustice. We know, because we have watched the process, that progress is so slow as often to seem nonexistent to younger observers. But we have observed that child labor was abolished along with twelve-hour workdays. The status of women and blacks is at least legally better. We seniors have seen these reforms in the making, perhaps had a part in their making. Hence, when a campaign of ours loses, we are not unnerved as the young so often are. We can be disappointed in an official or a legislature, but we don't despair. Unless we are just perversely pessimistic, we can see the enormous amount of energy now being spent on works of mercy and good will for the retarded, the disabled, the disadvantaged, the handicapped.

"Good works," we used to call such activities until the phrase fell into disrepute along with its slugging offspring, "do-gooders." But the efforts go on.

Or take another youthful illusion. Then we were told that money was all, and at the same time the root of all evil. But by our time of life we have noted two salient facts about money: All the troubles of any period of life are intensified or multiplied by the lack of it, but it alone won't rid anybody of any real trouble. When one has soaked up those two facts about money, he is not likely to be either overawed by it or contemptuous of it. Believe me, that bit of knowledge is very feeling!

We have also learned that no joy is without its price. Babies are still born in pain or at least discomfort. Success often comes bitterly slow and sometimes never at all. Loved ones sicken and die. Even the tenderest of relationships have their costs in anxiety and separation. Woe is always there in the wings, waiting to replace Joy at any minute. But who in his senses denies himself Joy because he may have to deal with Woe?

When one has been stripped of such illusions, he is free to enjoy as a gift every good thing that comes his way – and to accept the sure-to-come misfortunes as events to be expected, like rainy days and occasional spells of the flu. If there is such a quality as the "serenity of old age," I suspect it derives in good part from having shed many of our illusions. It's a painful, but very freeing, process.

9

Old Age Brings Opportunities for New Undertakings

FOR CULTIVATING THE MIND OR SOME SPECIAL BENT

I have remarked on the number of old people who are going back to school for a high school diploma or college degree. (When I was working in a literacy program in St. Louis, I discovered that an occasional old person goes back to acquire enough skill to "read my Bible.") In the mood of today and unless the inflation gets too bad, it is safe to predict that more and more middle-aged and old people will go back. Power to them. Even if they never get the degree or the diploma or never find a monetary "use" for it, they will have greatly bolstered their self-esteem, because they have proved that they "could do it." Almost all the comments of these late matriculants testify as to how terrified they were at first. Hobbled by the general view that old brains have necessarily deteriorated, they are desperately afraid of competing with "sharp young people." Just to be rid of that fear is a blessing, but proving to oneself that one still has a functioning brain is much, much more.

Going back to school is, however, far from being the only oldster ventures counted newsworthy. Mr. Raskin's file also includes stories of: a Cincinnatus, New York, man making his first sky dive at age 65 and still jumping when 75; A Mobile, Alabama, 80-year-old, having earned his diploma in radio and television repair, launching forth on his new career; an 87-year-old Pennsylvanian hiking the 261 miles of the Appalachian Long Trail in Vermont; a retired North Carolina banker and industrialist becoming a tennis pro at age 67; a 72-year-old doing pushups with 180 pounds strapped around his waist; a Chicago woman taking up both painting and swimming in her 70's and doing at least some of her swimming in cold Lake Michigan; another Chicagoan, aged 84, turning to a study of cuneiform inscriptions: another elderly Illinoisan becoming extravagantly involved in digs for Indian relics; and a fellow townswoman of mine, aged 78, making the St. Louis Post-Dispatch by bowling 196 after taking up the sport at age 72. According to the French ski champion, Killy, some of us are even going on the slopes. And of course there is the balloonist Jeanette Piccard and her fight to become an Episcopalian priest, and Sir Francis Chichester and his round-the-world sailing feat. Not to mention Rear Admiral Samuel Eliot Morison, who at 84 led a group on a 40,000 mile voyage retracing Magellan's first circumnavigation of the globe.

Few of us, of course, are so venturesome. Most of the activities we undertake are related to or perhaps derived from those with which we already have had some acquaintance, and involve little hazard to life or limb. Let me cite a few of these, all from my own circle of relatives or friends.

A former colleague of mine left the academic path into which he had been headed and became an accountant, ending up in the Howard Hughes organization. After retirement he set about an old dream of reading or rereading all the great novels in order to formulate his own theory of the novel as a work of art. Along with that ambitious project he began to write a series of auto-biographic novels of his own. Unfortunately, death caught him before he could finish, but he had a glorious time during those post-retirement years.

I know several people who have become at least near-expert in some field, not because they ever expect to use the knowledge, but simply because it interests them. Go into the reading room of any large public library and observe the number of elderly people with several books stacked in front of them and ball-point busy at notes. Most of these people do not expect ever to "use," that is, make money from the knowledge they are acquiring. They are simply interested in a field they never had time to explore in earlier years.

Genealogy, of course, is one of the favorite hunting grounds. It would be interesting to know how many genealogy buffs there are among our numbers. There must be thousands of them. I have a longtime friend now well into her 80's who chased her ancestors back through early Pennsylvania and then spent several summers in England tracking down still earlier ones. Among the male devotees of my acquaintance are a retired oil chemist in Tulsa and a retired engineer in St. Petersburg Beach – two professions one would think highly unlikely to produce the kind of sleuths who can happily pursue an ancestor through fading church and courthouse records. I am told by those who have experienced it that there are few triumphs more delicious than finally filling out a "line."

Other retired people are launching just as enthusiastically into the arts and crafts. Wherever there is even a moderate concentration of old people, there are classes in painting, pottery-making, needlecraft, and the like. Some of the products are sold in church bazaars or, if they are "folk art," in tourist shops. In many an elder's week, "my painting class" is the high spot. Not many of us turn out to be another Grandma Moses, but most of those who take this path have a high old time trying!

In a society like ours any ex-accountant or bookkeeper can find plenty to do either for part-time pay or gratis for an organization he happens to be interested in. More than that, in this day of public libraries, adult education courses and "interest groups," there is simply no reason why any senior who is reasonably intelligent and sound of wind and limb cannot find some interesting activity to undertake that he had no time or energy for during his working life. (No reason and, if you ask me, no excuse.) If he does find such an activity, it goes without saying that he will not be one of the old described by a cousin of mine, who is herself just entering old age: "I can now understand Mother D's reluctance to be with people her own age. I find so many people of my age can't talk about anything but their children and the past." Everybody knows the kind of seniors she is talking about, and we all spend as little time with them as we can.

TO HUNT NEW WAYS
TO BE USEFUL

Society in general, or at least large portions of it, may feel that we are surplus, a useless burden to be carried as gracefully as possible, but yet carried. It is plain jellyfishy of us to acquiesce in that view. Unless we are completely disabled we can pull at least a good part of our weight and be all the better for the effort.

Heaven and the sociologists know

that human needs and unsolved problems swarm horrendously out there beyond our doorsteps. They also know, and so should we, that we more than any other age group have both the experience and the leisure necessary for working on some of those problems. Their variety is so great that whatever our talents and tastes, a place can be found for them. (It is also known that sometimes our aches and pains will quiet down amazingly when we are out trying to tone down someone else's tribulations.) Heaven and the sociologists know all this. What has been lacking is, first, our own understanding of both the seriousness of the problems and the part we can play in working with them, and second, some kind of social machinery for gearing us efficiently into ways to help.

It will be my thesis in Part III that with the help of federal, state, and local governments and community organizations, my generation could pioneer in the development of the needed social structure to allow older people not only to have "second careers" (if they want them) but also to be as needed and useful as they ever were. At this point it is enough just to mention briefly some of the meaningful ways that a few of my friends have found to spend their retirement years.

Working with wood seems to be a favorite with male retirees. An orthopedic surgeon has turned his accomplished hands to making beautiful furniture and elegant boxes that will become heirlooms or perhaps even museum pieces. And there's a school administrator who began as a manual arts teacher and is now doing fine woodwork, using the equipment at the school where he had been working. And the executive who was forced into early retirement by an unreliable heart now contributes time and experience to counseling people setting up or running small businesses.

As I said earlier, my husband, who was a lawyer in labor relations, discovered before retirement that he had "good hands and a way with wood." Before his death five years after retirement, he was turning out really interesting pieces. His family treasures them, but the most important fact about them is that in those last five years no day was ever long enough for him.

Another acquaintance, an ex-newspaperman, made a new career for himself with a newsletter put out by a large volunteer organization. A man in his seventies went back to his high school Latin and began to write out a translation of Virgil. Another friend in her seventies began to work in a counseling program set up by her church. She had long ago majored in psychology and somewhat later worked with children in a juvenile court. Whatever academic psychology she had learned in the past was probably no longer in vogue. But she had brought up four children, had read and thought, and being old, she had had much experience. She turned out to be so valuable to the people who came for help that when the St. Petersburg Times decided to do a good-sized article on the counseling services available in the community, she was featured.

One of them, over eighty, has cultivated the ability to work well with younger people and to listen (both rather unusual abilities in the old!). As a result she does a good deal of informal counseling and has a respected voice in the affairs of her community. Several of my acquaintances who were formerly office workers have become administrative assistants in churches. Working part-time, for whatever salary can be paid and does not interfere with their Social Security status, they attend to the thousand and one details involved in the smooth running of any good-sized organization that has real estate to be maintained and a varied program to be coordinated. Another St. Louisan, Catherine Soraghen, was a teacher of social studies in one of the top high schools of the country. When she retired she was in good health and eager to try something new. For four years now she has been one of the "Wheels" in the St. Louis League of Women Voters. I doubt if she ever puts in less than a 30-hour week, and I know from hearing her say it that she feels as good about herself in her present job as she did when she was working for money. Before his death, Raymond White, a retired minister, took over a large part of the sick-calling in the church near his retirement home, thus giving his pastor more time for study. His age probably made him more useful to the ill, especially the terminally ill, than a younger person would have been. After all, he had had a long time in which to find out what comforts and what doesn't.

All of us know such seniors. But how universally they have been overlooked in all the outpourings about the pitiful, isolated old! Though most of them no longer hold or desire to hold official responsibilities, they are still active, and what is more, respected in the groups to which they belong. They go to lectures and "meetings." They do regular volunteer work in hospitals and service organizations. They lend helping hands to friends with problems of some sort – especially to their contemporaries or those somewhat older than themselves. When one of their circle becomes a widow or widower, they, the people who have "been there," are the first to come – and they are the most helpful.

In short, they lead busy, effective lives in spite of joints that creak a bit now and then. They don't envy the young or look back to the "good old days," which they well know were not always as good as some of their contemporaries like to let on. They are loved by their children and grandchildren. In spite of the limitations to which they are subject, they are probably as happy as they ever were.

In a careful study recently published by the National Institute of Mental Health, 47 men ranging in age from 65 to 97 years, averaging 71 years, were subjected to an exhaustive series of psychological and physical tests against a control group averaging 21 years of age. Five years later the same set of elders were brought back to undergo the same tests, with exception of 8 who had died, one who had moved to Florida, and one who "couldn't be bothered." Though the average age was now 76, they were still a lively group who had maintained their interests in people, ideas, and activities. Their physical appearance had changed little. Socially, most of them had expanded rather than retreated. In the psychological tests some did better than five years earlier, others not so well. Writing about the research in the United Methodist publication, Together, Edith M. Green summed it up thus: "We should keep in contact with other people, for the research highlighted that meaningful relationships with people warm the lives of individuals who age most successfully." The research seems to show that as long as old people are free of disease, maintain good relationships with friends and family, and make good use of their leisure, they will have a "good old age."[1] Old age doesn't have to be, it really doesn't have to be "pathetic."

But, someone may object, "The activities you're talking about belong to the early stages of old age, what Dr. Larsen calls 'the active period.' What about the time when we can't be so active, are in what she calls the 'sitting' or 'frail' period?"

Florida Scott-Maxwell used that period to keep a notebook from which emerged The Measure of My Days, perhaps the best book yet written on the experience of old age.

When she was ninety my fellow towns-woman, Edna Gellhorn, broke a hip that did not heal, and so had to spend her last two years sitting in a chair or lying on a bed. But during all that time, until she finally slipped into a coma, she "kept up" with public affairs, just as she had always done. She used her telephone and

1. The study is officially described in Human Aging: A Biological and Behavioral Study, U.S. Government Printing Office.

242

pen to make her views known to her mayor, governor, or legislator. But most of all she maintained her own superb spirit and interest in everything human. So greatly was she loved that people continued to come to her during the whole two years. Indeed, so many of us came that we learned to make appointments so that we would not tire her with too many callers in one day. But – and this is the real measure of her service – none of us ever came away from her without feeling enriched and somewhat fortified against the fear of what might happen to us in old age. She had the pain and the frustration, yes. But she also still had that on which she had built her courageous, compassionate life – the satisfaction of being useful. Not long before her accident she had spoken of "the boon of seeing that lengthening years need not keep one from loving and being loved." Perhaps she served as well during those two years of sitting as she had ever served. She heartened many of us who were back up the road a bit, gave us courage to face old age.

Or take a case even nearer to me. After an unusually bright business career one of my sisters, Hildred Dungan, had to retire early because of failing health. Though mostly housebound and usually pain-ridden, she got the books and trained herself to do instruction in remedial reading. For several years now she has been working with about eight first and second graders who have trouble learning to read. Usually they respond to the special attention (plus the cookies she keeps on hand to reward successes) and before long are back in the class before their self-images have been much damaged. How can anyone estimate what she has accomplished while sitting there in her apartment? Or, for that matter, what her life might have been without what she calls "my children"?

"But," another objects, "I'm just an ordinary person without the education or experience to do what such old people do." Perhaps so. But there are things to be done that almost anybody can manage. Perhaps he or she is able to join in what some communities call "the buddy system" and others call "telecare" or some such name. Each participant in the system obligates himself to call each day a list of housebound people who live alone, in order to make sure that they are all right. If there is no answer, someone from headquarters goes out to check. Eventually, caller and called may become "telephone friends," who look forward to the morning chat. All housebound, lonely old people who are thus contacted testify to the sense of security they have in knowing that in some emergency they will not be left alone indefinitely.

Letter writing to shut-in friends is another activity practically any "frail" senior can engage in. Most can manage to get to a senior citizen center, whose variety of activities contains at least a few attractive to them and suitable for their condition. The women's societies of many churches make a real effort to bring their frail members to meetings. A little imagination and determination are usually sufficient to turn up ways in which people in the later stages of old age can be highly serviceable to those around them. Even if one is literally and finally chairbound, he is not condemned to uselessness.

I have even known people who managed to be useful during the last or "bedfast" period. Of course the unfortunates who are kept in long comas by the hospital machines cannot perform any human service for those around them. But for others, those who are permitted to die naturally, even a long final illness does not rule out usefulness. My father-in-law, for instance, spent his last four years in bed, but at home. He was almost immobile, but fully conscious and in no great pain. From having been a driving, sometimes sharp-tongued, man he became a "model patient," grateful to those who cared for him. To all appearances he was not excessively unhappy during that long sojourn in bed. Sometimes, as when his minister came to call on him or one of his children came from another state, he experienced happiness. If he was at times depressed, he made an effort to conceal the fact. People said it was "an inspiration" to visit him. By his behavior he was demonstrating two facts about death and dying: They can be accepted and they do not necessarily rob one of his usefulness. To quote Dr. Birren again: "Everyone is too old for something, and no one is too old for everything."

In some lines of work one becomes "too old" at an early age. To Bob Gibson, for years the star pitcher on the St. Louis Cardinals, old age came at age 39, when he learned that henceforth he would never start a game, would only be a reliefer. He who for a whole season had averaged one earned run a game was to go into the "bull pen." When he told a sportswriter, "Knowing nobody wants me to pitch was the low point for me," he was expressing what many, perhaps most, employed people feel as that "great leveler," the sixty-fifth birthday, approaches. 'But events have proved that while he may have been too old to pitch, he was not too old for something else connected with the game.)

TO PERCIEVE ONE'S LIFE AS A WHOLE

In the last section we were talking about opportunities for growth and usefulness still open to us from the outside. We must now turn to the inside – to the opportunities for pleasure and growth through reflection. There are, I insist, such opportunities and we ignore them to our peril.

In old age we have for the first time a chance to think about our life as an evolved pattern, as almost a whole. Always hitherto we had to think of it in parts and as incomplete. As young children we could not do much more than react to the stimuli beating upon us from moment to moment. In the identity crisis of adolescence we learned to look back to our childhood and make judgments about our parents and the effect they and the other circumstances surrounding us had upon our development. In the overwhelming need to grow up we were apt to make harsh judgments upon both parents and the surrounding circumstances, such as poverty or lockstep schools. "If my home life and neighborhood had been difficult, I wouldn't be feeling so boxed-in" is the almost universal plaint of adolescents. Sometimes resentment and a desperate desire to break out of what seems to be the cramping cage creates a rebellion that the youth never quite outgrows and that leads to an almost total dependence upon peer groups for behavior guidance. (By which yardstick we all meet plenty of graying adolescents!) Or he may become one of the fiercely independent, aggressive loners never fully able to relate to anyone.

Later he may or may not come to realize that his negative reactions toward parents and surroundings influenced his choice of vocation and marriage partner. If he makes unfortunate choices in one or both fields, his whole life may be badly affected, and its ambience may become one of regret, either angry or sad. Because hardly any of us ever achieves what we dream of in youth, most of us have carried through the harassed middle years a secret load of self-reproachful sadness, even of guilt. Or, if we happen to be the active, unreflective type, we may have kept ourselves too steadily on the run to think much about how our lives were shaping up.

In old age we have at last the experience and the leisure to think about our life as a whole. And the necessity to think so of it, because how can we accept the fact of having grown old, of having already spent most of the coin dealt out to us, with nothing to show for it except a life that has been an assortment of bits and pieces instead of a meaningful whole?

More than two millennia ago, Cicero

proclaimed in his lofty rhetoric that "the harvest of old age is the recollection and abundance of blessings previously secured." It was a good metaphor. It really does seem like harvesting – gathering in the fruits of one's life – to look back over the years and see how this led to that and both to something else. That long childhood illness, for instance, could it have caused a tendency toward neurasthenia? And how did the Great Depression, which fell upon us just as we were getting well started, affect the later turns we took in political philosophy? How would life have been different if one's father had been less authoritarian – or less permissive? Less easygoing – or less ambitious? Or less any of the other qualities that made him what he was? And how did it happen that we got the right (or the not-so-right) marriage partner? How did that choice affect our whole life? What were our most serious mistakes, and how did they happen? How did our successes, such as they are, come about? Did we do about as well as could be expected with our life, given the ingredients originally placed in our hand?

There is a wonderful passage in Erikson's Identity, Youth and Crisis that sums up this whole line of thought so well that I quote it at length:[2]

In the aging person who has taken care of things and people and has adapted himself to the triumphs and disappointments of being, by necessity, the originator of others and the generator of things and ideas – only in him the fruit of the seven stages gradually ripens. I know no better word for it than integrity. . . . It is the acceptance of one's one and only life cycle and of the people who have become significant to it as something that had to be and that, by necessity, permitted of no substitutions. It thus means a new and different love of one's parents, free of the wish that they

2. Erik H. Erikson, Identity, Youth and Crisis, pp. 139-40.

should have been different, and an acceptance of the fact that one's life is one's own responsibility. It is a sense of comradeship with men and women of distant times and of different pursuits who have created orders and objects and sayings conveying human dignity and love.

Erikson uses the word "integrity," but it seems to me that he might as well have said "perspective." But by whatever name it is a quality we elders must have if we are to "age successfully." And if we are ever to develop the quality, we must win it now. It couldn't be had earlier, and we may not be granted time for it in the future.

Time changes our outlook. I was recently fascinated with a televised interview of Averell Harriman on his World War II dealings with Stalin, Roosevelt, and Churchill. Some of his comments on the three were, I'm sure, different from those he would have made in the Forties, even if he had been released from the constraints of diplomacy. Why? Because history had flowed and some of his perceptions had changed with his lengthening perspective.

And what are some of the "blessings previously secured?" In retrospect they may be quite different from what we thought when in the process of securing them. Most of us have had the experience of setting our hearts upon some achievement or honor and then not "making it." Sometimes in retrospect we discover that missing it was a blessing. Some relationships that we prized went sour on us. At the time the loss may have seemed catastrophic. Now we can prize what we learned from the suffering.

In memory, the joys of our child-rearing days remain joys, that is, blessings. But as seen in perspective the anxieties and the sorrows of that same child-rearing period are very different from what they were in the stresses of the moment. So much did "come out in the wash" that much of the fretting and nagging may now seem pointless or even absurd. In the same way, all the pain we suffered as we watched our children as young adults make what we thought serious mistakes now may seem to have been unnecessary pain. Or, on the other hand, that pain may have been only the first twinges of a heartache that lasted for years. It hurt, but perhaps we can now see that it taught us patience, or even a measure of openmindedness.

In any case, as we consider the present mutual affection that we and they have built in the long flow of time, the whole experience of parenthood can be knitted into a manageable whole. And much of what we resented in our own parents' attitudes and behavior can finally be understood and, if need be, forgiven in the light of how much we ourselves misunderstood or failed to understand in our own children. Thus the pattern comes to include the whole sweep of our generational life.

In other past activities the same gathering-in of blessings and acceptance of mistakes can go on. The joys remain joys, and the anxieties and frustrations should be accepted as having at least taught us a small amount of the ability to possess our souls in patience. At the very least we may have learned to be less certain of the godlike rightness of our views.

Perhaps the need to see one's life whole is why so many seniors are prompted to write what are called "memoirs" when celebrities do them. The rest of us do it half-apologetically, maybe secretly, because something we do not quite understand pushes us to try to bring all that happened to us into some kind of order and meaning. Even the passionate interest that some old people take in genealogy may spring from this need.

There is another homely rural metaphor for this assessment of oneself in the light of all that has happened to us: "The chickens have all come home to roost." Some of those chickens, like the "blessings of harvest," are absolutely delectable. But others are most unwelcome. If, for instance, we overate and underexercised during our earlier years, we are now probably prime candidates for heart disease. If we smoked too much, we may lose a lung or be cursed with emphysema. If we sacrificed everything to getting ahead, our particular chicken may be a bored, friendless old age, further plagued by indigestion.

No one in his senses will claim that the life of the virtuous old is free from mischance and suffering. We have all seen too many cases of magnificent human beings brought to the ignominy of near or complete senility. Just as we have seen people who were critical and judgmental become mellow in old age. But by and large, it does seem to be true that a lifetime spent in developing such qualities as courage, compassion, and a humorous appreciation of the human animal as "at once the slime and the glory of creation" helps to make endurable the physical and emotional pains of old age. And even to prevent some of those pains, if only because such a one has pleasanter things to think about than the coward or sourpuss can muster up. Beyond that, of course, he is far less likely to be lonely, because people don't mind being with him.

Even though nobody else (except perhaps young grandchildren) wants our recollections, they are a very precious harvest to us. Just to think of our past is to create a kind of awe before "all we have been through." Novelists have intuitively known about this awe, for they nearly always have portrayed the approach of death to an old person as a period when he retraces his long passage through time. The young and middle-aged are apt to disdain this preoccupation of the elderly as "living in the past." It can, of course, be that, if carried to extreme. But the need to assess the past and to some extent relive it is, I am finding, an important part of growing old.

Can it possibly be more than forty years since Franklin Roosevelt was telling us that all we had to fear was fear itself? Or more than thirty since Hiroshima shoved us trembling into the nuclear age? Such thoughts come to us in a mixture of pride and humility over having survived. Throughout all the tumult and the changes, we have been present and participating, however infinitesimally. What we have seen and felt, this generation of ours!

One of the most pleasurable parts of the remembering process is also unknown and impossible to earlier stages of life. For want of a better term, I call it "reflection on the rise and roll of the generations." Only we who are old can think of grandparents who lived through the horrors of the Civil War; of parents struggling against great odds to climb a few rungs up the American Ladder; of our own childhood with its joys and deep hurts; of our children's joys and pains intertwined with our own; of our grandchildren, so different from ourselves in manners and ideas; and, perhaps, of great grandchildren. What a procession to have come under one pair of eyes! We ourselves are nearing the end of our voyage, but so long as the generations keep coming on, there is hope for America and for the species.

So we remember – and wonder. (But only to ourselves or with close old friends! Our juniors scorn all such activities.)

TO GROW THROUGH ACCEPTANCE OF AGE

In our culture it is terribly difficult to accept the fact that one has become old. At every turn we are reminded that society does not respect us. At the very instant when we think we have gained ground in our "endless struggle to think well of ourselves," someone comments glowingly about how "sharp" a mutual acquaintance remains although he "must be past eighty." (Meaning, octogenarians are not expected to be "sharp.") Or our remarks in a meeting are heard politely and passed over quickly. Or our doctor attempts to comfort us by a hearty, "For your age, you're just fine."

Most of all, we keep noticing that we can no longer do something we were able to do, though perhaps with a little difficulty, only a year ago. Our short-term memory is failing. ("Where did I put my glasses? I had them right here only a minute ago.") The word we want may simply refuse to "come." Our slowing mental processes and muscular movements are making us feel insecure in heavy traffic. And so on. Any oldster can fill in the list. We do slow down. We do become unsteady and lose muscular strength. The chronic disabilities with their aches and pains do mount up. More and more often we are embarrassed by the signs of our aging.

In the face of all this how can anyone have the gall to talk about accepting old age as a means of growth? Especially when in common usage to "accept" something means opening a hand to take it. That is, saying "yes" to it. But even more especially, when common politeness requires that we say as we extend the hand, "Thank you." Gratitude for the condition of old age? How ridiculous can one get!

I want to be brutally clear about this. We are talking about "acceptance," not "resignation" and not "submission." About saying, "Yes, thank you," instead of "I submit because I have to." About not saying with Maurice Chevalier, "Considering the alternative, I like it fine." To accept old age because after a certain number of years death is its only alternative is not to accept it at all. Acceptance is saying, "Yes, I am growing older. It is happening now, today, and will continue to happen. I am grateful for the chance to experience it and the new opportunities it brings."

When we first begin to think of it, there is something very paradoxical about regarding old age as a time for growth, because any numbskull can see that it is a time for decline and decay. But it can also be a time for growth, for the final flowering of the personality. Always, in every generation, a few people have proved the possibility.

The law of Nature is that all life runs through a cycle. It is born, it grows, it matures, it declines, it dies. To fight the cycle is to ask for trouble. The child who does not grow is grieved over as "retarded." The youth who clings to his childhood may make a beguiling figure in a drama like Peter Pan, but in real life he is a horror. If he clings unduly to his adolescence, he is soon enough labeled "neurotic." And the adult who will not assume the burdens of maturity may be regarded only as a colorful oddball, or he may end up in a mental hospital, or even in a prison. Why should we, the old, be exempt from the inexorable demand that we keep moving forward? And from the demand that we accept the movement, even though our physical and mental powers are declining and will continue to do so?

But, someone objects, you have just been talking about the activities through which the old may continue to grow by cultivating the mind, seeking new ways to be of service, and so on. Why suddenly jump to talking about something that sounds suspiciously passive?

The answer is two-fold. First, activities are for as long as one can be active, usually until the early part of old age – for most of us now that is at least till the mid-seventies, for some the mid-eighties, for a few ninety and past. For all of us, for as long as we can be active, activities are a way of lengthening the active years while at the same time shoring up our sense of our own worth. But we all continue to decline. Inevitably, if we live long enough, we become "frail." (In my youth the usual Midwestern word for the state was "feeble.")

The second part of the answer to my shift from activity to acceptance may lie in my own experience. Because I have always by temperament been an activist and rationalist, with a scant amount of the contemplative in me, it is especially difficult for me to write about acceptance of this final phase in our life cycle. Like most Americans, I have always been in a hurry. I've been interested in causes, running hard to keep up with whatever procession I found myself in. Learning how to be old and accepting what values can be wrung from age do not come any easier to me than to other people. Consequently, for me it is much easier to talk about going back to school or becoming involved in volunteer service, those opportunities for growth possible to the senior who is still able to be active.

But I know that if I live to advanced old age, I shall probably become frail. In which case I shall have to give up most or all of the activities that now give me a somewhat useful role in the community. I may become house- or chair-bound. And even if this never happens, I am practically certain to be forced to progressively give up my outside activities, because I shall not be equal to them.

I should not kid myself about this. Unless I am to become one of the extraordinary oldsters who are still going strong at ninety-five (and by their very rarity make such good journalistic copy that everybody hears about them), the losses will keep on coming. Activity by activity, I may, or more likely shall, have to yield ground.

And while this is happening to me, I shall have to respect and like myself as I am then – and do it in the face of a society that says I am becoming progressively more useless and burdensome. Believe me, the cultivation of such self-respect takes a degree of ego strength that I'm not sure that I, any more than most other oldsters, possess. The cultivation of that self-respect is, I am coming to think, one of the primary tasks of old age. Also one of the chief means of continued growth.

How do we go about the task?

In the first place, we can look or try to look at the whole problem, and not just at part of it. Many students of age seem to agree that the common refusal to accept old age, indeed the common horror at the prospect of growing old, is rooted in our anxiety about death. Until we come to some sort of grips with this anxiety, it continually gnaws at us, consciously or unconsciously. By our time of life we have many times suffered losses at the hands of death. After watching helplessly while loved ones died, we have had to remake our broken lives. And always we have known that IT was lurking out there in the future for our own precious, feeling, being selves. Now, when we are old, we somehow have to absorb the idea that the day cannot be very distant.

In this respect man's task is, of course, infinitely harder than that of other animals. The entire problem for an animal is how to escape at the moment an enemy threatens. But throughout our entire history, man has had to try to deal with the knowledge of approaching death. Dence all the rituals, charms, magic, philosophies, and religions that our shamans, wise men, theologians, or Savior could devise to ease our fear. We moderns mostly attempt to cope by repressing the whole topic as much as possible. Because it touches us so deeply, we shy away from discussing it. Only recently have books been coming out with titles like On Death and Dying and Death With Dignity.

But in the end there is no way for us to avoid knowing that every day brings IT closer. Hence, one of the really important tasks of old age is to absorb the idea of death looming for oneself. Complete assimilation of the idea may be impossible, but whatever progress we can make will help to cushion this most basic of anxieties – while at the same time helping with the problems of loneliness and self-respect. If we can move cheerfully through our last allotment of time, and even with a degree of tranquillity, we shall not only feel easier ourselves but will help to allay the anxiety of those with whom we come in contact. As for self-esteem, how can one revere the whole mystery that is Life and at the same time respect a Self that cowers like a whipped spaniel at the very thought of the final Mystery?

How we go about the task of assimilating the idea of approaching death depends upon our own personality and upon our life circumstances. No matter how fruitful our lives have been, some of us who were brought up on the doctrines of eternal hell fire or even a long period in purgatory following a severe audit at Judgment Day may be especially fearful. Thus a devout Catholic neighbor of mine on her deathbed told her middle-aged daughter that she was terrified of facing God. The daughter replied gently, "But you love the Blessed Mother. She has always helped you over the hard places. She will take care of you now. Trust her." The next morning the dying woman said she was no longer afraid, and in a few hours was gone. Similarly, an old uncle of mine, dying of cancer, was terrorized by the prospect of the hell fires that had been preached to him in his youth. There is no knowing how many old people are still carrying about with them a load of half-buried fears once implanted in them in order to make them "good." One can hope that in the last quarter of the twentieth century most of us who are within the Christian tradition can feel that death completes one phase of existence and permits entrance into another.

At the other end of the scale, Bertrand Russell in his old age proclaimed, "I expect to rot in the grave."

In between Russell and the believing Christian are many variations, such as Florida Scott-Maxwell's: "I do not know what I believe about life after death; if it exists, I burn with interest, if not – well, I am tired."

The task of coming to terms with the idea of death is almost impossible for young people. The very idea of being snatched away in the midst of un-fulfilled dreams and unfinished work is totally bleak, and perhaps the young and the middle-aged are sensible in thinking of it as seldom as possible. But for us old people the situation is quite different.

Our work is almost done and our allotted time has almost run out. For us the assimilation of the idea of death is not only important, it is quite possible. Too many old people have gone peacefully into the Great Silence for us to doubt the possibility. Simeon was far from the only human being who has arrived at death feeling that he was being allowed to "depart in peace."

For myself one of the really important tasks of my old age has been to face the fact that death cannot be far down the road. Like most active moderns, I always pushed the idea back into a corner of my mind. (That was easy, for the idea always seemed unreal, anyway.) But six years ago, when my husband died, I was forced to stop and take a good look at the Enemy. My husband had been, in every sense of the word, an excellent human being. In my anguish I concluded that a life such as he had created simply could not have been waste material to be sloughed off casually by a heedless universe. From there I moved on to my own situation. I too had tried to live my life well. There had been mistakes and false starts galore. But my efforts had been both genuine and persistent. They and I would not be simply brushed into the trash can, not in a universe in which everything seems always to be in a process of transformation into something else. Goodness knows it was not a new idea, but it was comforting.

During this period I also came to understand in my very bones what is meant by the saying, "We all owe life one death." Gerald Heard's metaphors were also helpful: "Death sweeps Life's path, trims Life's lamp, lifts the husk from Life's faded flower." Without death Life would long ago have choked itself out. Thus it is only part of Life. Viewed in that way, death for the person I loved and for myself in prospect was much easier to face. I still do not relish the idea of having to die – there are too many books I haven't read and too many landscapes I haven't seen for me to be in any hurry about paying my debt to life. But I have, I think, said "yes" to the fact of my coming departure from the scene. It is possible, I am finding, to feel with E. Merrill Root,

Birth was the great adventure,
    and now death
Shall be the great adventure. We shall go
Beyond the bourne of knowledge
    and beyond
Time's one-way flow.

None of us can know ahead of time how well we shall perform in the supreme test of dying, because we cannot know how painful or how prolonged it will be. Or even how much mind and spirit we shall still have to work with. Nowadays, when the hospital life-support instruments and techniques can keep us alive long after our brains are dead, the effort to accept death's approach may be especially fearsome. Undoubtedly, it is for this reason that so many old people are now signing the

Euthanasia Educational Council's statement, which was included at the end of Part I. Taking this step may in itself help ease the facing up to death.

In any case, if learning to think of death as a fairly near prospect without at the same time becoming morbid or terror-stricken is not a means of "spiritual growth," then I do not know what those words mean.

And now back to the problem of withdrawals.

Gradually, over a period of months and years, or perhaps suddenly if he gets a heart attack or stroke, the piling years will eventually force the old person to make some withdrawals. His constant problem is to find just the right balance – the delicate optimum balance between activity and withdrawal. Hanging on too long will be just as bad for him as quitting too soon or too completely.

For a lively senior who has been hitting up a good pace, the shock of having to give up some of his new activities may be as severe as the shock of retirement was. Agonizing before a schedule that has become too tiring for his declining strength and is beginning to make him feel driven, he may argue to himself that he enjoys these activities. They constitute his last obvious social role. Must he really give them up? They confirm his social worth. How give them up? Can he keep part of them, or must the renunciation be total? (A question for his doctor, perhaps.) And finally, oh, here's the rub, if he really must give them all up, what can he find to substitute for his loss?

Such are the questions our gradual decline forces upon all of us, unless we chance to die before they strike us. Blessed are those of us who earlier acquired good decision-making techniques. Twice blessed are those in whom the I is strong enough to allow regarding ourselves and our struggles with a sensible portion of detachment. Such a one will be able to feel that even if he can no longer be a Foster Grandparent or Pink Lady or officer in a Senior Citizen

Center, he is still a part of the universe and so has an inalienable right to be in it. Nothing – not the disrespect of society, not his increasing physical and perhaps mental disabilities – can rob him of that right. If he can substitute the term "child of God," it will, I think, serve even better. But in either case he needn't think that once telling himself that he is a part of the Universe or child of God will do the job. Most likely he must keep reminding himself, and then he must be on the lookout for specific ways in which to validate his claim.

One way may be to pay some attention to the unlovely old person generally regarded at the center (or the church or in the neighborhood) as a Grade A pest. Or perhaps to call upon the hard-of-hearing, arthritic persons up the street, or give a sympathetic ear to the outpourings of an angry teenager. For a senior with a little imagination such opportunities are practically limitless. Unless done in a blatantly missionary spirit of "doing good," they can be not only useful but very reward-ing. The beauty of them is that until we are actually bedfast they are open to us no matter how frail we may become.

But to perform well in such ap-parently simple undertakings most of us will have to cultivate some new at-titudes. (Which is to say, continue to grow.) The ability to listen well does not just descend upon us with the coming of wrinkles. It is a skill that for most of us must be acquired, and in the early stages acquired at considerable cost. Who wouldn't find it more entertaining to play cards with one's friends than to sit down and listen to someone's troubles? We have plenty of those ourselves, don't we? And when we have submitted our-selves to sitting through the trouble-statement, then what? For those who, like me, are by nature prone to react with a quick burst of gilt-edged advice, attentive listening does not come easy. Take it from me, handing out advice is a lot easier than good listening.

Too many people "in conversation"

don't really listen at all. They are so eager for an opening that will allow them to get in their own "two bits worth" that they merely sit through the other person's remarks, scarcely hearing them at all. Or they are too impatient to tolerate the beginning small talk which the other person may need in order to be able to say what is really on his mind. But eventually, if his listener is patient, the person with a problem on his mind may be freed to show his true self, and perhaps even to work out a way to cope with his trouble. By the patience and skill of the listener, and not by the wisdom of the advice, is real counseling born.

I am discovering that when one becomes genuinely interested in the needful human beings around him (and everybody is needy in one respect or another), and when one tries to understand what others are like by listening to them with truly listening ears, many doors open. The condescension of Lady Bountiful or Lord Wise drops away, leaving room for something much more rewarding and conducive to our own personal growth. Instead of observing others from a height or distance, we begin to recognize the human plight of us all, and to yearn over the individual before us and over the poor dear old human race that is both the "glory and the slime of creation." This kind of combined participation and analysis is hard to describe briefly and harder to attain, but it is a wonderful plus that can be had in old age easier than before, because there is now more time to work toward it.

The secret is in our own attitudes. Because the word "love" has been so polluted as to be nearly meaningless as a motivation for the kind of listening in question, let's say rather, "affectionate concern for the other." That concern has always been considered to be one of the great means of personal growth. We do not lose opportunity to cultivate it just because we can no longer hold a job or even undertake a regular volunteer post.

What it requires is first, the time and the interest to listen and, second, learning how to listen. Psychiatrists and other professional counselors are taught the art. The rest of us mostly have to teach ourselves, with the help, perhaps, of some of Carl Rogers' books on client-centered therapy.

When she was seventy-eight a lifetime friend of mine, Orra Kuhlman of Corvallis, Oregon, wrote me: "My greatest joy in these last years has come in learning to listen – trying to understand and appreciate. It has become at least an avocation."

Two years later she commented in another letter:

Every year people, almost all people, become more interesting to me. I find myself engrossed in trying to understand what they are really saying, no matter what words they use. I used to classify them in my mind, but now I spend my time trying to dig them out of their pigeonholes. I used to argue with them inwardly, if not aloud, but now I keep trying to see what is in their ideas. Believe me, that makes being with people a lot more interesting than it used to be.

To reinforce those words for me, an almost-old cousin wrote me in her Christmas letter, "I'm finding that most people are not interested in my experiences, but very anxious to share theirs. So I let them, by listening." In so doing, she is rendering a service and no doubt has herself some quiet fun over the things that fall into her ears.

The art of listening has other dividends to be clipped. Apparently, everybody who ever wrote about successful aging bears down hard on the necessity to keep on acquiring new friends as well as new interests. It is terribly easy just to sit among our old friends who are no strain on us because we long ago learned all their likes and dislikes, ideas and prejudices, and so we can converse with them easily. But if we yield to that temptation we will become more and more isolated as the old friends die off. Somehow we have to keep right on making new friends. The surest way of doing that is through good listening. If we learn the art, some of the new friends may, glory be, just happen to be young.

To return for a minute to the advice-giving elder (or maybe to remind myself once more!), Paul Tournier thinks that the key to successful old age is in the "abandonment of the will to power." He adds that the difficulty of this abandonment is in direct proportion to the amount of power one had earlier. It may not be the key to all success, but it does appear to be the key to the unhappiness of the oldster who is great on giving advice but finds his gift unappreciated. He still wants to exercise control over the behavior and thinking of the people around him. But he no longer has that power, a fact well known to everybody around him if not to him. If he still attempts to use it, by showering them with his kernels of wisdom, they will try to keep a good distance from him. And his children, however bound to him in affection, will cultivate callouses on their eardrums.

Giving up the "will to power" does not come easy. When we were young we struggled mightily for that very power, were jealous of those who succeeded better than we in getting it, measured other people by their success or lack of success in getting it. What is more, most of us had a measure of power. Even if we never became an executive, office-holder, or foreman, all of us who were parents had it in almost absolute form for several years. Even those of us in the so-called "helping" professions, such as social workers and clergymen, measured our success in living at least partly by one or another of the power yardsticks.

Now we are old, and all of that hard-won power is denied us. As an organized group, we have a measure of political power. As individuals, we have little or none, except by the witness of our being.

If we can accept this deprivation, we are likely to be over the hump of accepting our age. Both those of us who insist on clinging to power by hanging on too long and those of us who give it up "because I have to" are surrendering a good part of our chance for a happy old age. But if we can give it up in the right manner, of our own volition, we do seem to be freed from some of the well-known curses of old age, as well as freed to live fully and happily in our last stage of life. To move from aiming for the next promotion to a stage where there will be no more promotions can be the occasion for bitterness. Or it can be the beginning of a new, but not less sweet, life pattern.

Those of us who purely love to hand out advice might try cultivating Mrs. Kuhlman's attitude and set ourselves to trying to understand others. Believing that despite our powerlessness we can continue to grow is at least one, if not the basic, avenue of growth left to us. Nobody is now under our control. Nobody has to obey us anymore – or yield us any deference. In fact, as we continue to move on into advanced old age, quite a lot of people may begin to give us advice, or perhaps even orders.

Understanding that we can continue to grow and to become despite our powerlessness is in itself an avenue of growth. If I keep harping on this matter of growth, it is because it is so important and yet not usually seen as a possibility for old people. If I could burn just one sentence into the mind and heart of everybody just entering old age it would be: Barring serious senility we can continue to grow right to the end. And I would add to that the fact that enough is known to prevent almost all cases of senility, if done in time. The great majority of us have a choice: We can become pains-in-the-neck or we can move on into a new phase of life that has opportunities of its own.

I have already given Pearl Buck's comment at age 79 that she believed herself to be a more valuable, more respect-worthy person than at any previous time in her life. Let me now go on with the rest of the quotation:[3]

I am a far more valuable person today than I was 50 years ago, or 40 years, or 30, 20, or even 10. I have learned so much since I was 70! I believe I can honestly say that I have learned more in the last 10 years than in any previous decade. This, I suppose, is because I have perfected my techniques, so that I no longer waste time in learning to do what I have to do. . . . Year by year we work for techniques in order to master ourselves and reach a growing understanding of ourselves and others. Happiness is based upon this primary understanding.

In reply to these remarks, it is easy to say, "That's all very well for Pearl Buck, a highly gifted person, one of the world's best known women. Maybe she could make such a statement. But the rest of us?"

3. Modern Maturity, Oct.-Nov. 1971.

What made the Buck remark stick with me is the fact that shortly before the article appeared I received a letter from Mrs. Kuhlman saying that she thought she was a better person than she had ever been before. (For many years we have been keeping each other posted on our little odysseys and musings about them. She was not boasting; she was just commenting on something she had noticed about herself.) Now she is most certainly not a celebrity. She is completely unknown beyond her own circle of friends and family. She was born on the lonely high plains of western Kansas, schooled in a small Methodist college and a pair of state universities, married to a professor on the low professional salaries of that period. She bore and hand-reared two children while doing her own housekeeping. She was early widowed and went back to another low-paid university job. She has more than her share of the disabilities of old age. On the surface she is an ordinary, obscure woman more than eighty years old. But she has been reading and thinking all her life.

I wrote her at once to ask why she thought she was a better person than in earlier periods. This is what she replied:

First, I like myself better. I have more sense. I am now sufficiently detached to have a different perspective. I have enough confidence in myself to be able to live alone and like it. I take my meals with gladness. In short, I enjoy myself. All this is new in the last ten years.

Second, my experiences are now more intense. This includes appreciation of beauty, color, line, harmony, melody, and the beauty of persons both outward and inward. I believe this is something that our losses force upon us. In the early months of my grief I took no pleasure in any of these things. About three years later I found myself enjoying the autumn colors again as I had never enjoyed them before.

Third, I have learned to be receptive

– to wait as we were once taught to wait for the leader's step in dancing, and be instant in following. It is a very intent receptiveness. I am not talking about something passive. I believe when we become interested listeners we are very precious to people. For a talker like me this is sometimes almost impossible. I want you to know it is a real achievement when I bring it off!

Maybe I should add that for me the sense of humor grows. I was taught that it is based on a sense of the absurd. I suppose it could be bitter, but mine isn't. I laugh at myself a great deal, and I laugh at our human efforts. . . . The old chagrin at failing is gone, and good riddance. This means I do not take myself too seriously and am therefore more easily able to forgive and forget.

Later in the letter she went on to comment on Dr. Larsen's remark that "we all learn to make substitutions to compensate the losses which are forced upon us by our advancing years." Her comment was, "I have never yet found a satisfactory substitute for anything lost. It is lost. And yet not, being held in memory and used. I have never searched for substitutes. It is more like exploring a new place within yourself or in the life around you that lands on your doorstep. You notice things you hadn't time to notice when your life was so full, and it sets you off on a new concern."

I have known Orra Kuhlman almost all my life, and so know that she was always bright, but that in youth she was rather timid and uncertain in her relationships. Perhaps even a little awkward in them. Now she attracts people of all ages and all mental outlooks. She really is a better person than she was sixty-five years ago when I first came to know her. Better even than ten years ago. Which is only to say: She continues to grow. And so can any of us. Dr. Herbert Klemme of the Menninger Foundation in Topeka, Kansas, has summed it up by saying that happiness in old age very largely depends on our working towards something rather than sliding downhill from our peak. "To be happy," he once wrote, "we must think of ourselves as in an unceasing process of becoming."

It is not an easy road to take, but it is a possible one. And if we can, in Mrs. Kuhlman's phrase, "bring it off," the personal rewards are very great. For then old age becomes a period as happy as any other. For most of us Dr. Klemme's are daring, unbelievable words. But there are among us those who demonstrate that it is not impossible to continue to grow right to the end.

Perhaps, and Dylan Thomas to the contrary, we should go gentle into the dark night. In that case we may even help a few of those in the next generation to face more openly the feared coming of that bogy – old age.

TO REAP THE FRUITS OF APPROACHING DEATH
The fruits of approaching death!

What kind of double-talk is that? Actually not double-talk at all, but the plainest kind of truth. A few pages back, we were talking about the importance of meeting the specter of approaching death head-on, instead of repressing it. I now go further and say that many old people are doing quite well at the task. One of the phenomena that has impressed me in these two years of talking intimately with the elderly is how few of them seem to be much bothered by the shortness of time left to them.

When I have asked them what they mind most about growing old, they have listed one or more of the following: "never being without some nagging ache or pain"; "losing my zest for living"; "being embarrassed by having my memory fail me"; "becoming so hard of hearing"; "losing some of my independence and knowing I'll probably lose more of it"; "fearing that I may become senile"; "being afraid I won't have enough money to see me out."

So far nobody has said, "Knowing

that I will die before long."

Of course it is possible that these people have so thoroughly repressed the idea of approaching death that it would take several sessions with a good psychiatrist to let them recognize it in themselves. Or perhaps they were like the old described by Samuel Butler when he said that they had lived so long under the shadow of death and had "so long found life to be an affair of being rather frightened than hurt" that they have become "like the people who live under Vesuvius."[4] That might account for part of their calm, but I think not all of it. I know many of these people well, and I simply do not believe that the idea of approaching death troubles them very much.

What the young and the middle-aged can't know is that once it is assimilated, the knowledge of approaching death has some good features. For one thing, the dwindling days become more precious.

4. Samuel Butler, The Way of All Flesh, Chapter 6.

As a nonagenarian of my acquaintance once replied tartly to a caller who had remarked that she would be glad when the dreary winter days were over: "When you're ninety, you don't wish any of them away." Many people in terminal illness have commented that the very fact that one's days are necessarily limited can sharpen appreciation of them. One friend said of the last year of her cancer-doomed husband's life: "It was the best year Willis and I ever had together." And Mrs. Kuhlman tells me, "My first thought in the morning is, 'I'm still here!' And then I thank Someone or Something. It seems like a gift and gifts must be acknowledged."

I myself have learned that the knowledge of time's limitation can help to balance the deterioration of the sense organs. My eyes may be somewhat dulled, but the stray thought that "this could be my last spring," sharpens almost to pain my response to swelling buds and the tender new green of opening leaves. My ears are considerably duller than they once were but the staccato chant of some neighbor children swinging a jump-rope in "hot pepper" rhythm is now pure joy, whereas earlier it might have been just "noise." I am one who has found it hard to endure what I consider the national disgraces of Vietnam and Watergate, but as I look out my study window at a fresh blanket of snow and a small tree full of chickadees and a few cardinals waiting their turn at the sunflower seed in the feeder below, I thrill to the knowledge that I am still part of the scene. I used to be too busy rushing around trying to improve the world to entertain any such thrill as those small, waiting creatures now give me. I am learning with the writer of Ecclesiastes to "withhold not my heart from any joy."

The sense of time's limitation is denied to the young – they think it is forever. But once that sense has been really taken into oneself, anything and everything are to be enjoyed. I have walked along a wide, white Gulf beach in Florida almost dazed by its sights and sounds. The hundred different shades of aqua running into each other from rippling surf out to the horizon and up into the sky; the sound of waves crashing in a storm or slipping lazily back and forth on the packed white sand; all the tiny creatures washed up from the depths and now about to become part of either the beach itself or of beachcombers' collections; the flocks of sandpipers running back and forth on their stiltlike little legs; the breeze against my face and the rhythmic movements of my body – not even when I was ten years old did my sense organs, dulled by time as they are, yield me more joy. Part of my bliss, I'm sure, I owe to my bone-deep knowledge that I may not be walking on this beach in another winter. Not that I often think consciously of the limitation. I don't. Only once in a while does the idea surface, and then not painfully.

Many things can stir this excitement for me. The sight of a blooming meadow or of a new moon sailing up right on schedule, the smell of a June garden, the birth of a late-springing grandchild or signs of a teenaged grandchild's maturation; an hour with a friend; the genesis of a new idea – anything and everything now come to me with a richness and poignancy they could not have when time stretched out apparently limitless.

One of the favorite literary metaphors for the aging process has always been "ripening." But in our society many of us don't seem to ripen very well. We fight old age instead of accepting it as the high point of the long years of growing and becoming. We tend to think of it as a shrinking, withering process, when the individual has had progressively to give up what makes life worth living until he is now no more than a dried leaf waiting for some wind to give it a final small tug. Perhaps the reason the concept of "ripening" is hard for us is because we are now so urbanized that many of us have never seen fruit ripening. But surely most of us must know at least a few elders who have become little islands of calm amidst all the storms of today. They have been through many storms and have developed courage and faith to deal with them. (Of course there are the others – the cantankerous, fearful oldsters who trumpet the evils of the day and add to everybody's burden.) The "ripe" old people also have their memories, but they know that the past was often brutally hard. But they survived, and now that time is "dwindling down" they are more able to enjoy the small boons that the days bring when one is on the alert for them.

In a way, such old people move on into an area beyond storms. Because they have come to a time beyond the pull of ambition and of the desire to bend circumstance to their will, they are beyond at least the fiercest part of the storms. Such old people do exist. Even under the pinch of poverty and disability they find ways to enjoy themselves and the life around them. They are one of our prime natural resources. The ones whom I have known were sought after by other people, including myself, as springs are sought out by the animals of the desert.

To repeat: The knowledge that time is "dwindling down" gives an added fillip to all our efforts to move ahead in the long struggle "to become."

One of the very special blessings of this last period comes to the fortunate old couples who are still jogging along together happily. Not all couples qualify, of course. Some of them bicker and grouse shamefully, and in fact seem actually to dislike each other. But if they have managed to create a good relationship while in the throes of life and both still have reasonably good health, these last years may be the very best they have ever had. Somewhere I have read that old age is the "final examination" that tells whether or not a marriage has been good. Whoever wrote that knew about the golden-wedding set. When the pressures of child-rearing and job are lifted, couples have time to plumb each other's depths and enjoy (yes, I said enjoy) each other's foibles. The complaints about Mary's getting bossier all the time or John's always being underfoot apply to some old couples, but by no means all.

For some this last period may be the tenderest that they have known, the most packed with daily enjoyment of each other's company. No honeymooner can be expected to believe it, but the easygoing companionship of these last years can be so deeply satisfying that those who have it wouldn't think of trading it for the drama and bliss of the early experience. And the knowledge that any month, any week may end their companionship is a real part of its enjoyment. A short time before his golden wedding, one of my brothers-in-law told me, "If Nelle were to die, it would be like having the tent pole ripped out – everything would collapse." An outsider might perceive the relationship of this particular couple to be like a placid little stream moving so quickly as to seem almost without movement. But to the participant the relationship was life itself.

Perhaps this is the place to return for a few more words about sex and aging. Most young people seem to think that lovemaking after sixty is not only rare, but when it does happen, they think it somewhat obscene. "Dirty old man" and "silly old woman" are standard epithets everywhere. I am told that whenever young or middle-aged men get together over a few beers one of the standard forms of humor has to do with the troubles of "old man" lovemaking. But the gerontologists are now undermining this particular brand of folk humor, because enough scientific studies now have been made to let us know that many if not most old couples are sexually active in their seventies – and beyond. And furthermore, that they enjoy their activity as fully, though probably not as often, as they ever did. A Duke University study that has been going for two decades indicates that two out of three men are sexually active past 65 and that one of five is still active in his 80's!

Women, they found, are less active, perhaps because so many of them are widows by age 65. But their interest and activity do not seem to fall off in later years.

As long as both partners are alive, nobody bothers. But when one of them dies and the other, in his or her loneliness begins to "make moves," the "children" are usually scandalized and may yank the elderly lover right out of his retirement home. But despite the filial protests, weddings do occur both in and out of retirement centers. As said earlier, one statistic has it that 35,000 elderly people remarry every year.

A recent television special discussed this matter of late love in considerable detail. The oldsters who were presented stoutly maintained that they had "fallen in love" just as surely as if they had been twenty. Some of them, the program went on to show, even set up house together without marrying, because they could not afford the cut in pensions that a marriage would cost them. This turn of events is a new twist in the general relaxation of sexual mores – and one we shall undoubtedly see more of, if the elderly population continues to increase and if the pension regulations continue to make weddings a luxury some elders cannot afford.

Because a few gerontologists and psychiatrists are also talking about the enduring need for tenderness and affection, the next ten years will undoubtedly see a good airing of the whole subject of love among the elderly, so that it will not be as it still mostly is, a subject for derisive jokes. We are born sexual creatures and apparently we die sexual creatures. At the very least, we never outgrow the need for tenderness and for affectionate companionship. For that reason the lives of elderly singles may seem thin and unsatisfying unless they make a real effort to satisfy their need, either through sublimation of some sort or through finding a new person with whom they can be close.

Meantime, let all old couples who still

can enjoy each other be thankful. One of the fruits of their knowledge of approaching separation is this special kind of companionship, the like of which cannot be known before the long years of linked lives have created it.

TO ACHIEVE RELIGIOUS GROWTH

Of all the compensations to be wrung from old age and dwindling time, growth in spiritual or religious stature must surely be the hardest to write about. It was not always so. At one time anyone who chose to talk or write about it had a body of accepted ideas to draw upon and the knowledge that the folk wisdom as well as a Sacred Book backed every word he would say. No longer. We live in a time of general cynicism about both the doctrines and the behavior of churches. It is also a time, particularly among those intellectuals who write and those who work for the media, of widespread disbelief in the Sacred Book as the purveyor of literal truth.

Yet the human being seems to be as unalterably religious as he is sexual. Pick holes in an established doctrine, and he invents another. Reason or laugh a bit of dogma or a religious practice out of popular favor and another promptly springs up. Stop people from revering the Apostles Creed on the grounds of its claim of the supernatural, and Spiritualism, Satanism, and dozens of new sects promptly come on stage.

Like everybody else, we oldsters have religious views and attitudes, although some of them may not be recognized as religious even by those who hold them. Ours are as various as those of everyone else. Some of us are rigidly dogmatic and creed-bound, some almost without dogma or creed. Like any other section of our pluralistic society, we run the whole range of religious thought: highly theistic and purely humanist, Christian and Jewish, fundamentalist and "liberal," silent Quaker and tongue-speaking Pentecostal, Christian Scientist and Greek Orthodox, a sprinkling of

Oriental religions – all these and many more have elderly adherents. How can one possibly generalize about the religious life of old people, when it comes in such bewildering variety?

In the face of such diversity it is downright rash for anyone but a professor of comparative religions to attempt to analyze what common basis they all have, and so perhaps to make some kind of a generalization about old people and religion. Let me be rash if not brash.

I think the majority of us (a large majority among the elders I happen to know) would agree that there is in the universe a Force or Power that is both Creator and Sustainer. Paul Tillich's phrase, "the ground of all being," is now in frequent use and is generally accepted by most theologians. Those of us who are "religious" believe in our ability to love and commune with this Force; that in some mysterious way it responds; that this communication between us is a shield against the blows of life and a help in solving the problems of life. We believe that if we seriously seek contact with the Creator-Sustainer, we discover within ourselves something that, if we cultivate it and listen to it, helps to guide us. Call it the Holy Spirit or whatever, we find it there and it guides us.

In addition, most "religious people" feel great reverence for the individuals who have embodied humanity at its best, such as Jesus and the Buddha, and try to pattern themselves after them, because they have towered so far above ordinary humanity in their nature and in their service. The majority of us would, I think, accept these statements as the basic fundamentals of religion, phrased very broadly.

Like other pursuits, the religious life is not one we can put off to the last minute and then hope for sudden proficiency. In due course the person who has spent a half century or more ignoring the life of the spirit or at most contenting himself with a perfunctory church membership, like everybody else gets to be old. Nobody need expect him to turn into a contemplative or a saint overnight, or even in the course of a year or two. Or for that matter, ever.

But it is my observation (and experience) that the senior who has been plugging away at the religious life over the years does indeed reap a special harvest in his old age. Not that there has been no earlier harvest, but that some special kinds of rewards have been a-building.

For one thing he is happier. No matter how much misfortune or failure he has suffered, if he feels that the Force that set the universe going and has sustained it through billions of years also set him going and sustains him, small as he is, he will find it much easier to feel that his own life has significance and meaning. As I said earlier, to feel oneself "part of the universe" or "child of God" is a big help in shoring up an elder's sense of his own worth when he lives surrounded by a society that doesn't see much worth in him. It is then much easier to feel that his life has significance and meaning.

One of the best statements I have seen concerning this reward is by A. H. Maslow:[5]

He feels simultaneously small because of the vastness of the universe, but also an important being because he is there in it by absolute right. He is part of the universe rather than a stranger to it or an intruder in it. The sense of belongingness can be very strongly reported here, as contrasted with the sense of ostracism, isolation, aloneness, rejection, of not having any roots, of belonging to no place in particular.

Maslow was writing about what is called "cosmic consciousness," but the words apply also to anyone who genuinely feels himself to be a child of God. The feeling is a real help in the hard business of maintaining self-esteem at a period of life when the general attitude is to deny the old person significance and value.

5. A. H. Maslow, The Farther Reaches of Human Nature.

The feeling that one can and does communicate with (not only be heard by but answered by) the Creator-Sustainer gives a kind of wonder and joy, as well as confidence in facing the uncertain future left to the old. These are very powerful emotions.

For another thing, the genuinely religious person finds it easier to face his limited future. Whether or not he believes in an afterlife, his religious life is a support vis-a-vis death. I am not going into the perennial arguments about immortality. But I do want to make two points.

The first concerns a statistical analysis of the lives and habits of very old people, done in 1960 by the Gallup organization. It studied a sampling (402 individuals) of the 29,000 Americans then 95 years of age or older. One of the questions asked was about happiness. Of the sampling, more than half felt that their lives had been "very happy" and another 42 percent felt they had been "fairly happy." "In general," concluded the authors, "our old people have been happy people, bright as chipmunks most of their lives. They have been happy with their wives and husbands, with their children, with their education, with their income and with their social status. . . . Above all, these oldsters have been happy with themselves."

Of the 402 individuals (of whom, remember, over 50 percent felt they had been very happy and another 42 percent fairly happy,) 73 percent said they had been "deeply religious" all their lives. The authors remark, rather nastily, that "their present nearness to death may be causing them to take out a sort of theological insurance." But the same authors also note that around 1860, when these people were being born, only 23 percent of Americans were church members, and hence that this group of ancients do seem to have been considerably more "religious" than their contemporaries. Is it pushing a thesis to see a connection between the happiness scores and the religious scores of the group? And, perhaps, of both scores with the unusual longevity of the group?

A life that has been "deeply religious" has not wasted much energy in worry or hate. Throughout the years it has probably been growing in the ability to love and to extend itself in the service of others. When old age comes to such people, they have habits of thinking and feeling that are a real bulwark against self-pity and isolation, those twin dangers for the old. And now that the stresses of the work-world have been lifted, there is leisure to pursue the spirit's promptings.

As for the future and the question mark that death sets all of us I would like to quote two authors who have been meaningful to me, and then set beside them our obscure housewife again.

The first is Florida Scott-Maxwell, writer and psychotherapist during her active years. When she was in her eighties, she kept a notebook in order to stay alive while sitting alone in her small London apartment. Later some of her musings were gathered into a small book, The Measure of My Days. **It is, of course, highly unusual for a person of her age to have both verbal facility and psychiatric experience. Said she:[6]**

I do not know what I believe about life after death; if it exists then I burn with interest, if not – well I am tired. I have endured the flame of living and that should be enough. But the experience of the Unconscious taught me that we are fed by great forces, and I know that I am in the hands of what seemed immortal."

Her teacher, Carl V. Jung, when in his eighties wrote in the same vein:[7]

Death is an important interest, especially to an aging person. To this end he ought to have a myth about death,

6. **Florida Scott-Maxwell,** The Measure of My Days, **p. 75.**
7. **Carl V. Jung,** Memories, Dreams, Reflections **(New York: Pantheon Books), p. 306.**

for reason shows him nothing but the dark pit into which he is descending. Myth, however, can conjure up other images for him. . . . If he believes in them, or greets them with some measure of credence, he is being just as right or just as wrong as some one who does not believe in them. But while the man who despairs marches toward nothingness, the one who has placed his faith in the archetype follows the tracks of life and lives right into his death. Both, to be sure, remain in uncertainty, but the one lives against his instincts, the other with them. [Italics mine.]

And finally Mrs. Kuhlman, who, when I showed her the two quotes above, replied in a letter:

I have my own "myth," which is very simple. It goes like this: There may be more consciousness after death. If so, I trust it to be fascinating, difficult, by and large good, and not beyond my power to cope with. My trust is based on what this life has been, so full of love in spite of the fact that it is at present unfashionable to believe in progress. On the other hand, perhaps my life has been just a spark from the fire of the Spirit and will be extinguished. If so, I will never know it. For as long as I know, I will be alive.

To me it seems impressive that these three octogenarians, one a towering intellectual giant, one of middle fame, and one known only to her friends, should turn toward death faces so similar in their calm as to seem almost different.

In this attempt to show that age does have some enormously worthwhile pluses, I have had to skim the surface, and not merely because of lack of space. More important than limited space is my lack of mastery of what is to be learned from the process of growing old. Much of it I have only begun to take in. But I have learned enough to know that there are values to be wrung from the process and that those values are not of the marketplace. Furthermore, that it is no shame to us that we are no longer in the marketplace except as consumers. We have, so to speak, graduated from it.

One of those values, as I have tried to show, is leisure. At last we have time enough actually to try doing some of the things we always claimed we wanted to do. There is also time enough for some high-class loafing: sitting drowsily in a garden, or sauntering on a beach at sunset, or going to a movie in the daytime, or reading a book guaranteed not to improve our character. All the modes of leisure are ours if we want them. Finally, and perhaps more important, we now have leisure to hunt our ways of being socially useful in spite of our superannuation.

Another of the new values now possible to us is something all of us oldsters are inclined to claim we have: perspective. (Or perhaps, if we are having a particularly large day, in the recesses of our own hearts we may even dare to call it "wisdom.") In any case it refers to the enormous amount of experience we have garnered. We have learned in our bones (or should have) that whether we are on the giving or the receiving end of it, kindness is better than unkindness – for the incontrovertible reason that it makes us feel better. In the same way we actually know that love yields better dividends than hate or envy. We have also had time to observe that hope for the human species is easier on the disposition than despair – and not really any harder to justify. We now have proof that pessimism is hard on our nerves and digestion as well as on bystanders. We have also had the chance to observe and to demonstrate that usefulness is possible, right to the end.

Having acquired such knowledge, we are likely to find within ourselves the strength to hold up our heads, even if we are generally held to be a social problem, and some of us downright nuisances.

Even if it turns out that we have a long, expensive final illness, we are entitled to think that we have paid our way if we have demonstrated in our own elderly persons these sorely needed social values.

Is this the celebrated "tranquillity of old age?" Perhaps. If so, it is nothing lightly gained, but a grace we have won in long struggle. In fact, life is one long struggle, lightened by enough small joys and triumphs to let us enjoy it most of the time. Or as Christina Rosetti said more poetically:[8]

Does the road wind uphill all the way?
    Yes, to the very end.
And does the journey take the whole
    long day?
    From dawn to dusk, my friend.

But what a wonderful day – even in the hours of storm and near exhaustion!

8. Christina Rossetti, Uphill.

Part III

10

A Fresh New Wind Is Blowing

In the preceding section we listed and described some of the new activities undertaken by some of today's elders. The list makes no pretense to being inclusive. It simply mentions some of the activities I have either observed or read about. I am under no illusion that it includes more than a fraction of the activities engaged in by our twenty-two millions. But the list does, I think, constitute a kind of omen of a new day coming for the old. Almost daily, now that I have begun to notice and to listen, I hear of yet another senior who has managed to find himself or herself a "second career" in an interesting and socially useful function.

But even at that, their number is only a tiny fraction of us. As the director of a senior citizen center told me the other day, "Some of our people have become so accustomed to being outside everything that when someone first brings them in here, they sit like zombies." To such people the idea that they might once again have a lively interest in the passing scene, much less be once more a functioning part of it, must seem like a fairy tale – a pleasant notion with no connection with reality. Indeed, the most basic function of the centers now proliferating everywhere is to coax old people who are on the way to isolation back into society again.

But as things stand today, only the better educated and least passive of old people can find themselves a second career. Add to these qualifications the possession of enough income to cover transportation and other out-of-pocket expense, and it is easy to see why comparatively few of today's elders can buck the general view that old people are a social burden.

But even if they are so lucky as to have

education, a somewhat stretchable income, and a good endowment of "push," these seniors until very recently had to make their own connections and beat out their own paths. What has been lacking is some sort of social framework that would make easier for the ordinary retiree with his new leisure to move easily and naturally into his new role as once, long ago, he moved from youth into his new role as a productive adult. **Then he was supported by all the general social values and framework. Then he was** expected **to get a job, marry, do community chores, and otherwise assume responsibility. There is no such support or expectation for the same person after he attends his retirement party!**

At the second great turning point in his life, he is quite likely to find that he is expected not **to assume any new responsibility for anything except being as small a nuisance as possible. Which, practically speaking, means getting up in the morning and filling his next sixteen**

hours with whatever he happens to find and want to do. From here on out he is to do only what he pleases and to confine himself pretty much to the company of his age-mates. If he is so lucky as to have a pension and some savings beyond his Social Security, it is now almost de rigueur for him to follow the retirement party with some travel, perhaps a trip to Europe or a swing around the country in a camper. Such a trip breaks the nine-to-five pattern beautifully. But afterwards, what? So far as society is concerned, he is not expected to do anything but hang around and not make trouble.

But hanging around is not the way it should be. Since 1954 Dr. E. W. Busse, Jr., chairman of the psychiatry department of Duke University Medical Center, has been conducting a research project on 260 persons over the age of 60. The project has convinced him that "the elderly must remain productive." Why? Because in order to be fully human, people must have self-esteem. And in a society where good self-images are mostly achieved through money, position, achievement, or some combination of the three, the retiree may soon slip into thinking of himself as a nothing or, at best, a has-been. After all, he has had a lifetime of accepting the prevailing belief that only paid employment and achievement through "getting up the ladder" are worthwhile activities. After that long indoctrination many old people cannot by themselves create their own new values – indeed they see no reason for creating them.

I am well aware that some of the more fervent of today's feminists are saying that 'volunteer work is demeaning' – that any work worth doing should have a monetary reward, a check at the end of a week or a month. This view I flatly deny out of my own experience and that of many of my acquaintances and friends. I never received a dollar for any detail of my long career in community service But the rewards in the way of political education, training and experience in administrative procedures, understanding of human motivations, acquisition of a few group skills, and improved self-image are immeasureable. Some of my life's activities have meant paychecks, some haven't. Some of both kinds of work were creative and fulfilling, and some were boring. I have been paid for writing and I have written or edited for the League of Women Voters with not a penny expected or received. Some of both kinds of writing was drudgery, some fascinating. For that matter, nobody ever paid me or most other women a penny to bring up children, but from my present vantage point that particular activity seems like the most rewarding of all my long life's varied doings. I am and always have been a contender for women's rights, but I simply do not believe that anything worth doing must be crowned with a paycheck. So long as society fulfills our real needs through some of its channels, we owe it a return.

For the old with meager resources, programs such as Foster Grandparents, which pay small salaries, are proper and necessary – and the salaries should be larger than they are. But I fail to see why the "comfortable" among us must have our efforts legitimized with cash. If the work is both interesting to the individual and useful to society, he and it have their reward.

Because this belief runs counter to the prevailing American value system, it may be a very hard one for old people to develop by and for themselves. The lucky few with genuine intellectual or artistic or recreational interests may never need to worry about developing new value systems. But the rest of us are at serious risk. Too many of us go to church to sit passively accepting the offerings of choir and pastor. Or go to a senior citizens' center like children to a party playing the games and eating the food someone has prepared for us. Only the exceptionally spunky old person can propel himself out into new under-takings. And so the old tend to sink into a more or less resentful acceptance of the general negative attitudes our society has toward them.

In the course of writing these pages, however, I have become convinced that something exciting has begun to happen. A new social framework is being built – one that will allow the old to have a new, interesting, and intensely useful social role or function.

If I am right, this is an event of great importance, not only for a society that is half-smothering in unmet needs that taxes seem unable to cover, but for the old themselves. What else could so greatly strengthen both their own self-respect and the respect in which they are held by others?

If my hunch is correct, my generation is pioneering, just as truly as were our great-grandparents when they set their faces West, or our grandparents when they headed their covered wagons towards the Great Plains. The recent flood of horror articles and books about the shabby treatment of the old have begun to have an effect. America is getting itself together to mend matters.

In this movement our own organizations are leading. They are not only rapidly learning how to do effective lobbying for members' material benefit, but they are pressing those members to stay in the mainstream instead of living in the past or slipping into isolation. Joining in this compassionate cajolery are community institutions, such as churches and libraries, offering free meeting places and other services. Institutions of higher learning are offering extension courses in the senior centers. And back of all are whole new categories of governmental support.

All of this is new within the last ten to fifteen years, most of it since 1965, when the Older Americans Act was passed by Congress. And not all of it has come about because politicians see us as a source of votes. A good part of it has come about because the best of the old have seen the need for it and have extended themselves to bring it about.

Though the movement is nationwide,

it is mostly concentrated in urban areas, probably because the need is not so great in the countryside or small towns. There the old are not only fewer in number, but less likely to become faceless. Within the metropolitan area of St. Louis, for example, are nearly 300,000 people 65 or more years old. Within the core of the city, 14 percent of the people are elderly. Both the impersonality of city life and our very numbers make us a sizable urban problem. Hence most of the work is being done in cities.

I shall concentrate on what is going on in the city I know at first hand. Because I have been poking into its centers and interviewing their program directors, I have a pretty good idea of what is going on in St. Louis. But there is no reason to suppose that our local senior scene differs significantly from that of other cities. For example, on my desk at the moment are recent news stories describing:

1. The We-Fix-It Committee of Lan-

caster, Pennsylvania, Chapter 530 of the AARP. This committee provides low-cost repair service to the chapter's membership of over 1,000 people, using the skills of some of its retired members. The fee is small, or nothing for those who can't afford to pay. The committee estimates that in its first five years it did 800 household repair jobs. (St. Louis once had a repair service of this sort. It "fixed up" not only the appliances but the houses of old people on an ability-to-pay basis.)

2. Project INSTEP (Integrated Nutritional and Social Services to Elderly Persons) in Pinellas County, Florida. With some public funding it recruited and trained volunteers to find the poverty-ridden, sick, or isolated old people in St. Petersburg and other communities in the county and then to help meet their needs, which might range all the way from food or medical attention to companionship. Volunteers engaged in the search and the assistance included

people who ranged in age from their 20's through their 70's.

3. In Knoxville, Tennessee, a retired businessman in his eighties got bored and set out to find something interesting to do. The Eastern State Psychiatric Hospital took him on as an unpaid employment officer. Now he spends 18 to 24 hours a week helping newly discharged patients find employment. Because of his many business contacts, he has probably been more successful than a younger person might have been. He estimates that in his first two years he found 150 jobs for people who might otherwise been unable to reenter the working world – and he "had fun" doing it.

In their first years of retirement, when they are still in what Dr. Larsen calls "the active period," older people all over the country are taking on heavy assignments in community organizations such as churches, health associations, neighborhood councils, agencies dealing with crime prevention, Planned Parenthood, the League of Women Voters, United Nations Association, and many others.

Throughout the country many retired teachers have taken some special training in remedial reading and are now tutoring disadvantaged children or those plagued with reading difficulties sometimes due to minimal brain damage.

Articles are beginning to appear on what is now being called "volunteerism." This is now a rapidly growing movement, though of course it is not really new. The struggling frontier settlements of which our history books make so much were dependent on what was really volunteer effort, though it was apt to go under the name of "neighborliness." Under frontier conditions some individuals developed special skills the neighborhood needed and felt free to use in return for little or no pay. Thus my Grandmother, who went to Kansas in 1866, became the neighborhood public health nurse and midwife. People felt free to use her and she never refused an emergency call, though she was paid only in surplus food, if the neighbor happened to have it. When the neighborhood was fully established, some church group, fraternal organization, or (considerably later) women's organization would get together to organize and raise the funds for a new library or other needed institution – and then furnish unpaid workers to help "keep it going."

But during the twentieth century we have been moving more and more into a system where individuals or groups push government to take on new services. The government then creates a new agency to render the service, hires specialists to staff the agency, and levies taxes to pay the specialists. In the past, in times of general emergency, such as a war, when more help had to be found quickly and there were not enough specialists around, women were urged to "help out." Some women enjoyed this work and continued with it when the emergency was over. With the organization of parent-teacher groups, unpaid work in and around schools became more general. And, of course, churches have always used large numbers of volunteers, though under the name of "laymen."

Even so, the total number of people working on a regular but unpaid basis until recently was quite small. The general pattern was for some layer of government – local, state, or federal – to establish, under pressure, an agency to meet a demonstrated need, staff it with paid personnel, and finance it through taxes.

But in this field things are rapidly changing, chiefly because perceived needs have been not merely increasing but multiplying. **Back in the '50s and '60s, for instance, the demands of foreign affairs were gobbling up taxes, at the same time automobiles were needing highways to run on, schools were needing more teachers and rooms to accommodate the Baby Boom, and cities were needing practically everything. But** also during that time taxpayers were becoming increasingly mulish about such local needs as they could control through their ability to turn down bond issues and local tax increases. Also at the same time social scientists and ordinary citizens were constantly finding critical new **needs.**

Let's look at just one of those newly perceived needs. Who before 1950 worried much about the kids who couldn't seem to do well in school? Their case was unfortunate, of course, because it usually condemned them to a lifetime of hard poorly paid labor. But such jobs needed to be filled – and why bother too much about the people in them? When, however, machines began taking over large numbers of those jobs just at the time when the earlier Baby Boom had produced unprecedented numbers of young people seeking to enter the labor market, when a welfare system was in full flower, and when taxpayers were growing more and more sullen, then the kids who couldn't seem to learn to read or write well or handle figures became extremely important! Especially when there wasn't money to pay enough remedial specialists – and there weren't even enough specialists.

I could list other needs newly seen as urgent, such as for prevention of drug abuse among young people. Or for the protection of an environment that has already been badly damaged. Or for a system of national health insurance. Or for corrections that really "correct." Or for rebuilding our cities. Or for better nutrition among several segments of the population. The list goes on and on. We who are old know that in our lifetime there has never been a period when so many critically needed new services were waiting on the agenda. We may lament or applaud, but it seems to be true that much of what is important in good living must now come through organized social channels rather than from individual or even group action.

At the same time and in the same society, about two million people reach

65 every year, a good number of them with education, work skills and a considerable amount of residual ginger. Some of them are happy to "get shed of it all," others would like to find paid employment. All, I think, want to do something satisfying with the ten to fifteen years that they may now reasonably hope to have left. The lucky or the wise among them have provided themselves with an interest that may soon take them into what amounts to a second career. The ones who simply want to rock and fish soon get bored and settle stodgily into "being old." Those who want paid employment are not likely to find it. But given reasonable physical and mental health, most of them by stirring about can find volunteer activities that are needed and interesting.

Such a pairing of needs is a natural! And what is more, communities are beginning to come up with imaginative programs for doing the pairing. No wonder conferences are beginning to be held and books to be written about the selection, training, and supervision of good volunteers. There is even talk about "professionalizing" them.

As always, when a new social phenomenon is appearing, a new social structure begins to flounder into existence. With all the needs and all the elderly people looking for something interesting and useful to do, the machinery begins to be created, a bit here and some more there. Within ten years, I predict, the new retiree will be supported, just as he was when he emerged from adolescence, in his movement through what is almost a rite of passage into an interesting, useful old age. Almost unrecognized, a good beginning has already been made.

If the elderly person looking for some way to volunteer his services can't find it by himself, the chances are increasingly good that same agency can help him find it. A wonderful illustration of this new tendency for institutions to see how two needy groups can be brought together to their mutual benefit may be seen in the Ft. Smith (Arkansas) "Love to Share" program. Like all cities, large or small, Ft. Smith has its quota of "latchkey kids." Needless to say, because their parents are employed and nobody is home to greet them when they return from school, these children get into trouble. On the other hand Ft. Smith has its share of lonely old people who have too little income.

A local agency, Family Service-Traveler's Aid, brought the two needs together. A small federal grant was secured from ACTION and a project center was established in a church. After school the latchkey kids come there, drawn by the promise of cookies and games and the affectionate concern of the two old people scheduled that day to serve them as teacher and friend. For this the oldsters are paid $1.60 an hour, a sum their meager budgets can use. But the real reward to them is that they are, as one of them said, "Back in the world again, doing something needed."

When the federal money runs out, as it will in due time, it is inconceivable that Ft. Smith will not somehow find a way to keep the center going – and perhaps open others. Already some other communities have been inquiring about the "love to share" formula.

THE FEDERAL ROLE

The controversial Office of Economic Opportunity (OEO) seems to have been the first important step taken toward giving federal backing to community attempts to "get together to solve some of our local problems." Whatever their faults, the community action programs of OEO gave real impetus to people trying to improve the conditions affecting their lives.

When the decision was made to abolish OEO, a new, independent agency called ACTION was set up in July, 1971, to pull together a variety of the volunteer-oriented organizations then being sponsored by the federal government. Among these were the Peace

Corps, organized in 1963, VISTA and SCORE organized in 1964, and Foster Grand-parents in 1965.

The young agency boldly proclaimed its intention to be "a first step toward creation of a nationwide system of voluntary citizen service." To this end it aims to provide "centralized coordination and administration of an enhanced public image ... of voluntary services." Mike Balzano, dynamic director of the agency, intends that initiatives for new programs shall come from the local communities, not Washington. There are ten regional offices around the country. Much of the funding of the local projects is done either through ACTION itself or through Title III amendments to the Older Americans Act, but the local communities are required to make some contribution and to be prepared to take over full financial responsibility eventually.

From their beginnings both the Peace Corps and VISTA (Volunteers in Service to America) accepted elderly volunteers. Most of these did well with their assignments and enjoyed them in spite of whatever hardships were involved. Of course the most celebrated of the elderly Corpsmen was "Miz Lillian" Carter, who at 68 was working in a medical dispensary in India. But a not-young friend of mine was accepted, took her strenuous training, and went to India to teach villagers the fundamentals of nutrition, public health, and gardening – subjects she had learned about as a housewife and volunteer in St. Louis. And a retired Peoria, Illinois, teacher has had three tours with the Corps. After her stints in Liberia, India, Jamaica, and Lesotho, she was saying at age 77 that she hoped ACTION would find a new spot for her. According to the most recent Peace Corps figures 4 percent of its volunteers were over 50 – and 5 of them between 70 and 80!

VISTA, also, enrolled some elderly people in Puerto Rico and the Virgin Islands, and in our mainland slums and ghettos, Indian reservations, migrant camps, and institutions for the mentally ill or handicapped.

Because in recent years both agencies have been favoring applicants with specific skills and experience, the elderly now have a natural advantage toward acceptance. Quite a number of craftsmen, farmers, engineers, building-trades workers, or other skilled elders have found a crowning life-experience in one of these agencies. According to an editor and recruiting specialist at ACTION, "About half of the VISTA success stories have always been about older volunteers, even though they have never at any time accounted for more than thirteen percent of the VISTAs".[1] In January, 1976, the agency had 258 volunteers who were 65 years old or older.

The Foster Grandparents program got good press and is now well known. By August, 1973, a total of 10,500 elderly volunteers were at work with children in hospitals, training schools, day-care

1. Retirement Living, August, 1973.

centers, and the like. For working with two children, two hours a day, five days a week, the Grandparents are paid $1,-670 a year, plus transportation, noon meal, and an annual physical examination. To qualify they must have a low income and they must really like children. The institutions in which they work have been enthusiastic about the benefits their presence has brought to the children. In fiscal 1975, 13,627 Grandparents were serving 34,000 children. At the same time they were creating in themselves a sense of growth and self worth.

A less well-known, relatively new program is the Senior Companions. This program offers to adults, especially elderly adults, something like the kind of service the Grandparents provide for children. The Companions are selected, trained, and given a small stipend to serve in hospitals, nursing homes, intermediate care facilities, and various other settings related to health and welfare. By the end of fiscal 1976, the Companions are expected to include more than 2,000 volunteers working four hours a day, five days a week, to serve about 4,000 adults in 36 local projects.

All of these programs have been attractive and valuable to many seniors, but I think that RSVP (Retired Senior Volunteer Programs) is the one most capable of indefinite expansion. In its first year (1971), it had only 11 projects and 3,000 volunteers. By midsummer, 1973, it had more than 18,000 volunteers. By fiscal 1975, it had 666 projects and 149,000 volunteers.

Although RSVP offers no wages, it does have a paid-up accident policy for volunteers on duty and will furnish money for transportation, lunch, and other out-of-pocket costs if these are necessary. Its stated purpose is to offer "older adults a recognized and useful role within the community and through volunteer service, a meaningful life of retirement." Its projects are planned and operated at the local level and developed under the auspices of an established organization able to generate local financial support. There are no educational or financial qualifications and no upper age limits. In a study made of the volunteers more than half of those interviewed indicated that they felt better physically and nearly four-fifths of them said they felt better mentally because of the experience.

The volunteers work in many ways and many places. Their "stations" are almost any place in which a public or nonprofit group is at work. (Some idea of the possibilities of RSVP appears in the list of public and voluntary organizations to which grants were made during its first year: City Departments of Parks and Recreation, City Departments of Welfare, Community Action programs, Cooperative Extension Programs, Council of Jewish Women, County Bureau of Aging, County Department of Parks and Recreation, County Housing Authority, County Mental Health Services, Family Living Council of Health Associations,

Junior Colleges, Planning Councils, Settlement Houses, Volunteer Service Agencies, Volunteer Bureaus, and the Y.M.C.A. More recently hospitals, corrections institutions, day-care centers, and public schools have been making good use of the RSVP.)

If I can judge by what is happening in St. Louis, many thousands of elderly volunteers must be at work in schools. (In Saturday Review, February, 1973, someone propounded the theory that volunteers might tip the balance for our beleaguered school systems.) In just the ordinary routines of my life I have come across seniors working in nursing homes, senior citizen centers, hospitals, and quite an array of other service organizations. In Chicago some of them have been involved in an ACTION project to find foreign-born individuals and groups who may be isolated by language difficulties as well as by poverty. In the senior citizen centers the volunteers do clerical work, help serve the noon meals, act as hostesses, teach crafts, operate projectors – in short, turn their hands to just about anything required to keep the centers going. Another service often rendered is clerical work for nonprofit organizations such as the heart and other health organizations. Frequently the materials are sent out to senior residences, and those performing the work can socialize at the same time.

RSVP is, I think, a real jewel of an idea. It calls on the best features of the American character, and heaven knows that in every American community there are plenty of tasks needing to be done that are not likely ever to rate tax expenditures. But I suspect that, valuable and needed as the services are, their chief value is in making many seniors feel needed again. Especially since many of the organizations require careful training. St. Louis County, for instance, gives 60 hours of training to its volunteers for duty in its juvenile court system. Those hours are probably equivalent to a college course.

SCORE (Senior Corps of Retired

Executives) and ACE (Active Corps of Executives) differ from the other volunteer groupings in that they are composed only of executives, either retired or still active. SCORE was originally sponsored and operated by the Small Business Administration, and both groups have now been shifted back to that agency. Both are composed of volunteers who have had or still have successful careers and are willing to share their knowledge and experience with small businessmen in need of help.

Again I say it: Volunteerism is a natural for America.

THE STATES

Activity in the field of aging is fairly new to the states, and I have made no particular study of it. A few of the new state programs have, however, come to my attention, and the following jottings show some of the diverse directions in which the states are moving. Most states now have agencies called "Commission (or Office) on Aging," or something similar. These serve as channels through which some of the federal funds are funneled to local communities. But, like the other levels of government, states are also developing programs of their own – programs that are more than "handouts to keep the old folks quiet." Although, of course, the fact that we are more likely than other age groups to find our way to the polling places must occasionally stray into the minds of state official-dom.

Some states, perhaps by now a majority of them, have passed what are popularly called "circuit breaker" laws to give lower income elderly home owners and renters credit on their state income taxes for a proportion of what they have paid in homestead taxes or rent. The hope is that such seniors will thereby be enabled to stay in their own homes and neighborhoods, instead of having to be herded off to some dismal rooming house or "home."

Other innovations are coming. Missouri, for instance, in setting up a Home Health Care program used a voluntary organization, the Missouri Association for Social Welfare, to seek out agencies around the state qualified to take health care into the homes of the elderly. When the system is in full operation, it will help to prevent the painful uprooting of many old people from their familiar surroundings. Many RSVP volunteers will undoubtedly be involved in such efforts to make the lives of some of their contemporaries more bearable.

Like many other states, Missouri was shocked to discover that according to some estimates more than 400,000 of its older citizens are malnourished. Their problem is not only lack of money, but also that many of them find it easier to open a can of soup than to cook a balanced meal and then eat it alone. Because undernourished people age faster than those who are well-nourished and are more likely to become a bedfast responsibility, Missouri and other states

are acting from more than simple compassion – and the nutrition programs for
the elderly multiply.

Along with its other programs on
aging, Colorado was one of the first, if
not the first, states to open up its university tuition-free to daytime students 60
or more years of age. While there is no
direct connection between this step and
the volunteer movement, the fact is that
old people with the desire and the energy
to undertake college courses at an un-
orthodox age are also likely to be
enthusiastic volunteers. Simply because
they are more mettlesome, they are more
likely to have scouted out interesting
volunteer activities. Although such
seniors are unlikely ever to show up at a
senior citizen center, they are quite likely
to have found a volunteer post at a
juvenile court or a bookmobile project
to reach the homebound. Having found
it, they are much more likely to work at it
enthusiastically than would those to
whom such a daring scheme as
enrollment at a university would

never have occurred.[2]

In its Department of Public Welfare, Pennsylvania has a fairly new Bureau for the Aging. According to its director, Robert Benedict, one of its "major thrusts will be to establish comprehensive services for the aging on a country basis throughout the Commonwealth." To that end regional councils have been formed, with the function of reporting their finding of needs to an Advisory Committee on Aging which in turn transmits the findings on to the appropriate state agency. In this way Governor Shapp hopes that programs on aging "will no longer 'belong' to one department or another," but to the people.

Pennsylvania's ambitious Community Services Program, or CSP as it is usually known, is well established, operating on an impressive number of fronts, one of which, needless to say, is

2. Several other states have taken the "tuition-free to the elderly" step; community colleges have been particularly active in the field.

aging. Since tax money is not likely to be found to cover the many-sided program the state has espoused, it will surely have to enlist the efforts of many hundreds of volunteers.

Arkansas is attacking the health problems of its elderly with a new mobile project called CASA (Community Activities for Senior Arkansans). This program gave free medical checkups to 10,000 elderly citizens and found 60 percent of them needing medical attention. So the state then began to send out into its cities and countryside a bus with testing equipment, two nurses, and laboratory technicians. The hope is to reduce or prevent chronic illness. The basic goal of the program is to provide medical assistance to the rural elderly in areas where there are no hospitals and sometimes not even any doctors. But the buses also go into poverty-ridden urban neighborhoods. Tests for blood pressure, heart functioning, lung capacity, and vision are given and the results reviewed by doctors. People with health problems are then advised to secure an appointment with their nearest physician. In rural communities the mobile units are scheduled a month in advance, so that older people can learn about them and make plans. As everybody knows, Arkansas is not a state with a high per capita income. But it, like Missouri, is beginning to understand that not only compassion but hard fiscal sense is involved in cutting down chronic illness among its elderly.

LOCAL GOVERNMENTS

Perhaps I can best describe what urban communities are beginning to do for their elderly by describing what is going on in my own city, St. Louis. Our projects may be no more numerous or imaginative than those of other cities, but I have been able to explore them. I have come out of my little survey impressed. In St. Louis the elderly are being drawn back into the community, and a social fabric is being created to give them a place and a role, if that is what they desire. And this in spite of the fact that St. Louis is having a notoriously bad case of inner-city blues. In the discussion that follows I make no pretense to inclusiveness with regard to the work of any of the agencies or institutions. All I am trying to do is give a general idea of what is going on in St. Louis, and therefore, presumably, in other cities.

The Mayor's Office for Senior Citizens

One thing the city had in its favor during the early days of its efforts was a Jesuit sociologist, commonly known around town as "Father Lu," whose brother Alfonso was then mayor. Lucius Cervantes, S.J., Ph.D., became the first head of what is now formally called the Mayor's Office for Senior Citizens, but is generally known as the VIP Center. He was posted off to Washington to garner whatever grants could be had. When his brother failed to be elected to a third term in 1973, his successor kept the VIP Center and retained Father Cervantes, who has continued to be an efficient garnerer. In 1973 the city contributed 25 percent of the program funds "in cash or in kind" and squeezed $60,-000 out of the revenue sharing funds. The rest came from the federal government via the State of Missouri.

It happened that the city owned an old downtown building that contained a big barnlike space formerly used as a bus station. A glass north wall, much white paint, a quantity of blue carpeting, and some orange furniture transformed dreary empty space into a cheerful, welcoming area. It is open Monday through Friday and is one of the busiest, happiest places I know. After becoming a nutrition site it was, by early 1974, serving a substantial noon meal to about 100 people for 50 cents or whatever the senior could pay. In September, 1976, some 300 persons were being served daily, besides the 900 meals being delivered out to homes or to 22 nutrition sites. Legal Aid counselors are available one day a week. A weekly Bingo game brings in a few hundred hopefuls. Card games and movie projectors are part of the scene. Sewing classes and instruction in crafts are available and some of the products are sold on the premises. In fact, I have never been in the place when it wasn't jumping.

The recreational program is diverse, including bus trips using the center's minibuses to ball games, concerts, and other local attractions, all at reduced entrance fees. In the fall there are apple-picking jaunts to the orchards of southern Illinois. Those who wish to venture further abroad can visit the French colonial houses at Ste. Genevieve, the state capitols of Missouri or Illinois, the Michigan tulip festival, or the Kentucky Lakes area. Sometimes available are such jaunts as a trip to the Grand Old Opry at Nashville. Real adventurers with the money and the vigor can take a bus tour of Florida or even a 7-day Caribbean cruise.

One of the activities being pushed is the "Home Security Program," funded by the Department of Agriculture and sponsored by the National Council on the Aging, Inc. If requested by an elderly householder, officers from the police and fire departments will inspect his premises for burglary and fire hazards, and prescribe what needs to be done to make the premises "secure." Then workmen under the direction of journeymen building-trades workers come out to make what changes are needed for security. New locks, carpentry and plumbing repairs, painting, perhaps a new toilet, winterization, general cleaning up, even grass cutting are available to improve the premises. The householder pays only for the materials used, and even those will be provided if he has no money for them. About 150 new jobs are involved in the program, as well as training in the necessary skills.

As would be expected, RSVP personnel are on the scene, a total of about 325 of them. They do all sorts of things: deliver meals or cook at the outlying centers, work in preschool centers and in lower grades at schools, help in a telephone reassurance program, and provide many other services. The AARP furnishes a good number of part-time clerical and other workers. Some persons with no specific skills are acquiring them.

In short, the St. Louis VIP Center is a highly visible, very useful effort to deal with some of the problems confronting older people. For several hundred seniors it is providing an interest in life, a partial answer to problems, and a social role.

The Cardinal Ritter Institute

Another large and effective agency in St. Louis is the Cardinal Ritter Institute. It grew out of the work the Catholic Charities of Greater St. Louis was doing among the elderly, and became that organization's Department of Aging in 1960. In 1962 it was accepted as an agency in the United Way (called "United Fund" in some cities). In 1965 its name was changed to its present form. It works in the fields of health, housing, income, provision of social role, employment, nursing home placement, relationship or personal adjustment problems.

In 1975 it served more than 14,000 elderly people and spent a total of $1,371,669 from federal and local sources. During the same year it bought a midtown Holiday Inn and converted it into the San Luis Apartments, with office space for itself and 226 dwelling units for the elderly. It also manages and furnishes services at five public housing sites, a suburban apartment development with nearly 200 units for elderly tenants, and a senior residence that was once a downtown hotel. As can be seen, its program is large and varied, but for our purposes, its most important work falls into two closely related categories, income maintenance services and the volunteer programs.

The institute has two types of the former services, Foster Grandparents and Senior Aides. Under the Grandparent program 86 low-income elderly people work with individual children in six of the metropolitan area's institutions for children, with the usual benefits resulting for both receiver and giver of affectionate attention.

The Senior Aides program furnishes part-time employment to 66 low-income seniors at $2.70 an hour. They work in various capacities at 34 sites and under the supervision of 12 different service agencies. Of these volunteers, 14 are health and hospital aides; an equal number help with transportation chores; 21 are in social service; 8 do clerical work; and 9 are nutrition aides. The institute selects and trains both the Grandparents and the Aides. Both types of income production not only help stretch pitifully tight budgets but give the senior a social role in which he can both learn and feel himself a part of the ongoing working world.

To combat the loneliness and boredom that afflict too many elderly people, the Institute supervises three different volunteer programs. The first, called "Friendly Visitors," consists of trained volunteers assigned to make regular, personal visits to aged and chronically ill people, usually those living in the volunteer's own neighborhoods. The volunteer's first responsibility is to relieve loneliness by "visiting" with his "friend," but he or she also can shop, drive, and otherwise function as a friend. In the fall of 1976, 263 of these Friendly Visitors were serving 528 persons.

In the Phone-a-Friend program, 44 elderly volunteers make daily phone calls to 49 old people who live alone and are often frightened and anxious. The daily call serves the double purpose of social contact and assurance that help will be coming if an emergency occurs. (Too many old people living alone worry for fear "I might fall and break a hip and nobody would find me for days.")

The third of the programs is our old friend, the RSVP. As usual, financial assistance is available for transportation and noon meal if the volunteer needs it. There are 427 senior volunteers now active in the institute's RSVP; they are serving in 52 different agencies and institutions throughout the metropolitan area.

The Jewish Community Centers Association

In St. Louis, Jewish groups were pioneers in working with and for older people. When most of their older people had moved from the city to the suburbs, a chief community center was built in a close suburb with a large Jewish population. Recently, as the migration still continued outward, a handsome new center building was built. On the same grounds was constructed Covenant House, a 100-unit apartment complex for the elderly, with another building of similar-size already underway. Much of what has been called "Senior Adult Programs' has been transferred to Covenant House. Because of the suburban setting and the difficulty of transportation for old people, the JCCA has an especially good minibus program. No Jewish senior has to sit home unless he wants to! All of the center's program groups are represented on the Senior Adult Council.

The regular, ongoing programs include:

An information and referral service to which almost any problem can be taken and from which help will probably be forthcoming.

A library, open five days a week, at Covenant House.

Social clubs, whose members get low-cost transportation to and from the center. Two or three groups meet (and maybe eat!) every day except Saturday.

Excursions and trips to historical sites and tourist attractions in Missouri and Illinois. "Culture trips" to the "Muni Opera" in the summer and to art exhibitions and a repertoire theatre in the

366

winter. All in the center's buses. Once a year there is a "pilgrimage" to Israel.

A variety of adult education courses – health lectures, arts and crafts classes, and gym classes.

Low-cost meals. (Lots of them, although the center is not a Nutrition Site.) Lunches and dinners are served as part of the programs of the various clubs that meet in the center.

Social Action. The Legislative program includes lobbying for Senior Citizen interests.

Volunteer programs. The center has its version of Foster Grandparents: a number of old people helping regularly in the center's day-care program. Also volunteers do two days a week of regular visiting in hospitals and nursing homes, with transportation in the center's buses. The director of the centers believes that one of its best features is the community service about 10 percent of its 1,000 older members are doing for nonprofit agencies. Each year the center honors these volunteers at a special meeting.

So far as I know, no public funding is involved in these services to the elderly.

Oasis

Although it maintains a pleasant headquarters in the office and community building of the Christ Church Cathedral (Episcopalian), the Older Adults Special Issues Society, or as it is always called in St. Louis, OASIS, has no church roots. It began as a kind of federation of Golden Age and Senior Citizen clubs. These affiliates now number about 150 groups located in St. Louis and its suburbs. A recent president, Mrs. Loretta Johnson, is well known in St. Louis for her year-in, year-out work on behalf of consumers. She fervently believes that people who get the short end of any stick should squawk, but should do it intelligently.

Her predecessors and the current president agree with her completely. Hence, whenever a hearing is being held in Jefferson City on some legislation of special interest to older people, a delegation from OASIS is sure to be in attendance and to make itself well heard. Its lobbying is, because of long experience, quite sophisticated. Some idea of its political potency appears in the fact that it puts out some 3,000 newsletters to dues-paying seniors.

One afternoon a month, every club and center sends in a representative to compare notes and ideas. The director, Dorothy Watson, herself a lively senior, is obviously happy in her work. Funding is small and comes through the Mayor's Office on Aging. The Cathedral also helps to fund by charging $25 a month for the commodious quarters. These include office space and a large, comfortable meeting place where parties and committee meetings are held and people meet to chat or play cards. Behind this room is the arts and crafts room, where classes are held and from which exhibits move to the meeting room.

Because the organization's chief function is legislative, it attracts and holds a special type of person – lively, intelligent, and not easily overawed.

The Urban League

As the Jewish people moved their centers to the suburbs, the Urban League took over their Center for the Aged in North St. Louis, and renamed it Tower Village. Its facilities include apartments, clinic, dental and podiatrist offices, and a good kitchen. Other equipment includes a small kitchen where the elderly residents can cook, a potter's wheel and kiln, an enameling kiln, and a woodworking shop.

Within recent years the Urban League has also taken over and renovated a large apartment hotel in the west central part of the city. Many retired people now live in the building and in nearby public housing. What had been the dining area has been converted into a Senior Citizen Center, complete with minibuses, weekly Bingo or Prokeno, a nutrition site, craft classes, free movies, and even a pool table in the hope of luring more men onto the scene.

When I asked about volunteering, the director told me, "These are mostly working class people, and they take the position that they worked hard all their lives and now they just want to rest." (This was corroborated by the Older Adult Program at the Episcopalian Grace Hill House: "By the time working class people get old, they feel too tired and worn out to take on any new activity.") But of course these were only generalizations. Some workers have plenty of energy left. For instance, in 1973 the small town of Nokomos, Illinois, got itself a handsome new 4,000-square-foot community building in spite of having only $25,000 in its fund. It happened because ten retired citizens, calling themselves the "Over the Hill Gang" worked a year under the direction of a retired bricklayer and a retired carpenter and cabinetmaker.

Other Activities

Scattered throughout the city is an array of Neighborhood Houses, (or in the older term, "settlements") all of which have programs for the elderly. In North St. Louis, for instance, five of these houses are part of Consolidated Neighborhood Services, with headquarters at Grace Hill, the Episcopalian House. All provide meeting rooms and dining facilities for senior groups and organizations. All are Nutrition Sites and the scene of varied social activities that help protect the old from isolation and fear in this low-income, high crime area.

At Grace Hill, for instance, six different Nibble and Chat groups meet regularly. Another group that calls itself the Get Together Club also meets there. Meals are served to over 100 people at the house plus to a good many shut-ins through a Meals-on-Wheels program. A Foster Grandparents program was tried once but did not succeed. RSVP fared better. About 26 people help out regularly. At Grace Hill activities vary from Bible study to tours on chartered buses to volunteer work in one of the five centers. At Wesley House more than 60 meals are served daily, and in its RSVP program, eleven men and women help out as needed. This help may be in maintenance, transportation, teaching in arts and crafts or sewing classes, or serving as receptionists.

Kingdom House, the Methodist operation on the Near South Side, sponsors a Golden Age Club that meets twice a month. Meals are served to about 75 people daily. Its RSVP has a group of about 20 people who help put out mailings in the center. About 50 others help in the day-care center, used clothing shop, and in serving the meals. They also do chores at the nearby City Hospital and a good deal of friendly visiting in the neighborhood. In fact, they seem to turn their hands to whatever jobs seem most needed at the moment.

Guardian Angel Settlement, a Catholic neighborhood house also on the Near South Side, in a primarily black area, sponsors two "meet and eat" clubs on different days of the week, plus a "Drop-in Lounge" open Monday through Friday afternoons. The Nutrition Site for this area is at a nearby senior citizen residence owned by the Housing Authority. The director of Guardian Angel told me, "Black people don't care much about games. They like to do things."

There are many other neighborhood houses in St. Louis and similar houses in other cities throughout the United States. They are, as every urbanite knows, part of the urban scene – and a real bulwark for the elderly person in danger of isolation, boredom, anxiety, and poor self-esteem.

Part IV

11

Summing Up

During these months I have been trying to look at the whole picture of old age as it is now being experienced in these United States. I have become considerably less pessimistic than when I first began to write.

It is, of course, still true that for many, old age is a miserable time. Continuing inflation adds to the torment, even though Social Security payments are now tied to the cost of living. It is also unhappily true that pain and/or isolation intensify the wretchedness of many old people, even the fortunate who have reasonably good incomes. In spite of all the research and the present knowledge about the prevention of arteriosclerosis, some of us continue to get strokes, and every nursing home has its living dead –

those whose very existence makes the rest of us anxious. And it remains true that none of us can know for certain that we shan't be sick or housebound in a few years or even a few weeks.

Some of the unpleasantnesses of old age are with us to stay. Barring a wholly new breakthrough in the research laboratories, we are still going to lose vigor and agility and mourn their departure. Despite good medical attention and careful handling of our physical resources, our eyes and ears will probably continue to dull. Unless we are willing and sufficiently affluent to resort to surgery, our faces will go right on sagging into new or deeper wrinkles. Too many nursing homes are still furnishing neither decent nursing or "home," and the good ones are out of financial reach for far too many of us.

All this remains true. And maybe will always be true. But nevertheless, the horror magazine articles and books are less true now than they were only a few years back. They served a good purpose and thank heaven for them, but one needn't be a professional optimist to feel that a better day is on the horizon.

Item One. **An angry chorus of voices continues to deplore the shabby treatment of many of the sick, isolated, and poverty-stricken old.**

Item Two. **In laboratories around the world, scientists are working on the causes and prevention of heart failure, high blood pressure, arteriosclerosis, cancer, and all the other plagues of the old. Already enough knowledge is available to make a big dent in those plagues, if we cooperate intelligently with our doctors. But, perhaps even more important, the medical profession is beginning to realize that conditions that had passed for senility and were thought untreatable may be only symptoms of medically manageable diseases, such as hydrocephalus, depression, atherosclerosis, inefficient heart action, anemia, hypertension, malnutrition, emphysema, and perhaps other diseases.**

Item Three. **Several relatively new**

organizations of the elderly are scrambling for better treatment for their members, and at the same time are pushing those members into new activities.

Item Four. The beginning of a social framework in which the old can find a place and a function for themselves seems to be appearing. And on every hand a new emphasis is being placed on the importance of cultivating "interests" long before retirement day.

Each of the four items is a fairly new phenomenon in this country. In each there is hope. But the most hopeful part of the picture is the fact that we, the old, have begun to see our own responsibility in the whole matter. If we meekly succumb to the current view that we are useless baggage left over from our "productive" years, we are lost. The best of us and our organizations now understand this basic fact. But while it is presently perceived by only a fraction of us, every month seems to find more of us catching on.

Responsibility means, first and always, accepting the fact of having become old – of being in the last stage of life, which is very different from the earlier ones, but not less important. It means that for our own and for society's sake, we fight the bogey of old age. Not merely old age itself, but the fearsome specter that has haunted us from youth. It means that we must keep (or win) our self-respect in whatever ways it can be kept or won. For me, one of the best ways is to remind myself occasionally that I am still part of the universe even if my hair is gray and my wits no longer entirely dependable. Because I have my place in the universe, I do not have to rot away in dread or self-pity. Perhaps this is really only another statement for the Judeo-Christian bedrock: "I am a child of God and am therefore entitled to respect from myself and from others." Whatever phrasing works best for a particular oldster is his to use.

Because I am as much a part of a stupefyingly complex yet unified cosmos as are the birds and the cirrus clouds visible from my city windows, I do not need to apologize for my existence no matter how "old" I become. I do not need to scorn my present phase. My contemporaries and I have as much right to be here now as we did back in the time when we were "doing the world's work."

But simply because we are part of the species, we must seek out the ways still open to us for picking up our share of the human tab. The United States has apparently embarked on the process of making it easier for us to find the way, but in the end only we can test out the ways. No amount of worthwhile volunteer opportunites and no number of compassionate agency directors can do anything much for us if we sink ourselves passively into the infantile entertainment provided for us by some of our would-be benefactors, or, worse, if we retreat to a self-pitying vision of the good old days. (Sure, we had energy to burn in those days, but we also had passions and ambitions that not only burned it wastefully, but tore us apart in the burning.)

That stage of life is gone. Forever. What we have to deal with now is a completely different state, demanding different life strategies. As Carl Jung said: "It is impossible to live through the evening of life with the programs appropriate to the morning, since what had great importance then will have very little now, and the truth of the morning will be the error of the evening. " It is up to us to find the strategies appropriate to the evening.

For myself, I find the scales constantly coming into new balances to which I must reconcile myself and from which I must extract whatever value they can be made to yield. The balance changes a little each year and each month, and every time it shifts I must make a new adjustment to my situation. Thus far I have been able to make some kind of adaptation to each new turn of events. As my eyes age, I have to be more choosy about my reading. As my ears slack off, I have to don the hearing aid I hate for its distortions. If I live, at some time in the not too distant future I shall have to give up driving – and in that loss become more dependent on family and friends. (And how we seniors cherish our independence! For many of us it is the fiercest passion we have left.)

As for the Event that sits somewhere out on the horizon, who knows how or when it will come? Best leave it and its arrival to Time, Fate, God, or whatever word one chooses to use. But unless it is too painful or too long and drawn out, most old people manage to get through it with a fair amount of grace, and likely so shall we. If we haven't lived like cowards, we are not apt to die like cowards.

As I have tried to point out, there are values to be had from old age. Real, undeniable pluses. In our society they don't hit us over the head. We have to seek them out, think about them, and put them to the test of practice. But they exist, and they can be sought.

And we don't need either to think of

ourselves as useless or to be useless. All kinds of needs are around us, some of which we are peculiarly fitted to meet. If we are determined, most of us can be useful until we fall into a coma on that last hospital bed. Lending an ear to the troubles of someone else can be enormously helpful. Even a telephone call to someone in a bad spot can be a form of usefulness and sometimes a real service. And cheerfulness is always a boon to those around us. What we absolutely must not do is to give up our interest in experiencing this last stage of life and in wringing from it whatever value can be extracted.

Above all, we must continue to grow. To stop growing is to die, even if we keep on breathing and eating. But barring serious brain damage or other physical disaster, we can continue to grow. Our generation is lucky in that a whole series of medical procedures and new social patterns and opportunities are coming into being just as we need them. As Fr. Lucius Cervantes once told me, only half-joking, "Old people are becoming the 'in group.'"

We are getting more attention and that attention is more intelligent than any former generation of oldsters ever had the luck to receive. We shall, of course, continue to have grievous losses, but there are substitutions to be made for most of them. The new agencies will help us find the substitutions or, as I prefer to think of them, the new balances. But the prime responsibility for making them is still ours. Although the senses and the joints have declined and probably will decline further, the spirit can still grow. Right to the final coma. I know this to be true because I have lived close to people who somehow managed to accomplish it. Their service to me has been incalculable.

Perhaps Robert Louis Stevenson said it best in Lay Morals: "So long as we love, we serve; so long as we are loved by others, I would almost say we are indispensable."

As I have tried to show, at least until

we are housebound the opportunities to be useful, though probably unpaid, are practically unlimited. Even when we can no longer get about much, we need not be useless. Our old friends die or move away, but finding and serving new ones can still go on.

But first we must accept the fact of having become old and set ourselves to the tasks that enable us to make the most of this last stage of life. One of these is to believe in the marrow of our bones that this last stage can be enjoyable and useful and that we can continue to grow in it. Shakespeare and his genius to the contrary, it is most decidedly not "second childhood and mere oblivion, sans teeth, sans eyes, sans taste, sans everything."

The other task is to create for ourselves a set of values that will allow us to respect ourselves in a society whose prime values are youth and "getting ahead." This society will not, and, at least in the foreseeable future perhaps, cannot create our values for us. If we are to have them, we must work them out for ourselves. Fortunately, the great minds and spirits of history have always been proclaiming them. In our younger days we ourselves may even have given them lip service. Now we must grasp them and make them our own.

In the evening there are stars that cannot be seen in the daytime. There really are.

The publishers hope that this book has given you enjoyable reading. Large Print Books are specially designed to be as easy to see and hold as possible. If you wish a complete list of our books, please ask at your local library or write directly to: John Curley & Associates, Inc. P.O. Box 37, South Yarmouth Massachusetts, 02664